TOUR

OF THE

GRAND JUNCTION,

ILLUSTRATED IN A

SERIES OF ENGRAVINGS;

WITH AN

𝕳istorical and 𝕿opographical 𝕯escription

OF THOSE PARTS OF THE COUNTIES OF

MIDDLESEX,

HERTFORDSHIRE, BUCKINGHAMSHIRE,

BEDFORDSHIRE, AND NORTHAMPTONSHIRE,

Through which the Canal passes.

———◆———

BY J. HASSELL.

" Thrice happy he, who always can indulge
This pleasing feast of fancy; who, replete
With rich ideas, can arrange their charms
As his own genius prompts—creating thus
A novel whole."

GILPIN.

London:

PRINTED FOR J. HASSELL, 27, RICHARD-STREET,
ISLINGTON ;
And sold by all Booksellers.

———

1819.

Ashridge, Herts, seat of the Earl of Bridgewater.

Drawn by I. Hassell.

TO THE

NOBLEMEN AND GENTLEMEN,

PROPRIETORS

OF THE

GRAND JUNCTION CANAL;

THIS WORK

IS INSCRIBED,

BY THEIR MOST OBEDIENT HUMBLE SERVANT,

J. HASSELL.

PREFACE.

TOWARDS the termination of our recent Tour of Picturesque Rides and Walks thirty miles round London, we fell in with a small portion of the country through which the Grand Junction navigation courses its way. The beautiful scenery which accompanied its banks, determined us to retrace our steps as far back as the town of Tring, to observe if a continuance of interesting scenery was likely to attend the stream, in its further passage from that town; to our gratification, we found it from thence, meandering through a country profuse with the picturesque, lined on its right with the Chiltern

Hills, and on the opposite side of the valley with a succession of wooded eminences, terminating the prospect with the bold knolls in the vicinity of Leighton. The abundance of timber, with church towers and spires, rising above the summit of the woods, gave a chearful variety to the vale beneath. We afterwards found the navigation directing its course through scenes of undiminished beauty, and replete with delightful prospects, uniformly picturesque, and sometimes grand.

Deviating from the tedious monotony of the turnpike road, the course of the stream destined for inland navigation must necessarily be directed through a succession of the richest scenery—whether stealing through the glades and glooms of rural retirement, winding round the brows of hills, or gliding through the vallies by which they are surrounded, alternately visiting the recesses of pictorial abode, or the populous town, and the busy "hum of men."

Such are the particulars of the Grand Junction navigation, we have undertaken to describe; which embraces a variety far exceeding that afforded by many rivers, as combining all the beauties of landscape—the elegance and splendour of the mansion and the villa—and the venerable remains of antiquity; nor have we omitted to combine the biographical anecdote, the historical record, or the critical researches on antiquarian topography.

In 1818, the annual gross revenue of the canal amounted to the sum of £170,000; it possesses 1400 proprietors; and its shares of £100 have recently sold at from £240 to £250 each. Many of the first capitalists in the kingdom are its proprietors, and its usual routine of business is so conducted as to give satisfaction to all who are connected with it.

We have exerted ourselves to combine the *utile et dulce,* and to embellish our descriptions with accurate delineations of the scenery which we have sketched on the spot.

TOUR

OF

THE GRAND JUNCTION

NAVIGATION.

IN contemplating the works of art and genius, we are very naturally led to admire the effusions of talent and comprehensive minds: these upon reflection produce stupendous ideas, which only want the fostering hand of patronage to render them subservient to national advantages.

To the discriminating judgement and liberal patronage of the late Duke of Bridgewater, we are partly indebted for the memorable services of the celebrated Mr. Brindley, whose undertakings, with peculiar satisfaction, we are about to present to our readers. This gentleman's whole life appears to have been occupied in study, and the advantages the public have derived from his works can well attest the result of his capacious understanding.

Inland navigation, to a manufacturing country, is the very heart's blood and soul of commerce, nor can we easily estimate the utility and importance of this mode of conveyance, in obviating the expense and tediousness of land carriage, or the more protracted delays invariably attendant on opposite winds and tides.

Canals in this country are of very recent origin. According to the best authority, the first navigable canal was planned and formed in Lancashire, and is still known by the name of the Sankey.

The Sankey Canal Company consisted of several gentlemen and merchants, who obtained an act of parliament in 1755, authorizing them to make Sankey-brook navigable from the Mersey river, which it joins, to near St. Helen's. The proprietors in 1761, by a new act, obtained an enlargement of their former powers, and then completed their object. By this last act they were empowered also to make a canal to extend from a place called *Fiddler's-ferry*, on the river Mersey, to a spot about 250 yards from the lowest lock of the Sankey. This new part is nearly two miles in length, and an additional charge of 2*d*. per ton is added to that of 10*d*. which was allowed by the first act of parliament. Hence it is evident that canals had their beginning in England from the success attendant on the Sankey; the spirit of enterprize and speculation began to extend itself in a multiplicity of similar works in other countries. A description of this canal is given by Dr. Aikin, in his History of Manchester, which we conceive it will be acceptable to our readers here to introduce. "It runs entirely separated " from Sankey brook, except crossing and mixing with it " in one place, about two miles from Sankey bridges. " Its length from Fiddler's ferry to where it separates into " three branches is 9¼ miles. From thence it is carried " to Penny bridge and Gerrard's bridge, without going " further; but from Boardman's bridge it runs nearly to " the limits of 2,000 yards, making the whole distance " from the Mersey 11½ miles. There are eight single and " two double locks upon the canal, and the fall of water " is about 60 feet. The chief article carried upon it is

" coal, of which, in the year 1771, by an account given
" to parliament, there were taken to Liverpool 45,568
" tons, and to Warrington, Northwich, and other places
" 44,152 tons. There are, besides slate brought down,
" corn, deal-balk, paving and lime-stone carried up.
" This navigation is never obstructed by floods, and
" seldom for any length of time by frosts. The highest
" spring-tides rise within a foot of the level at the canal
" at the lowest lock.

" Loaded vessels are generally neaped about three
" days; but unloaded ones can pass to and from the
" river at every tide. The old lock by which at first it
" communicated with Sankey brook, still remains, but is
" seldom used, unless when a number of vessels are about
" entering from the Mersey at once; in which case some
" of the hindmost often sail for Sankey brook, in order
" to get before the others. This canal has proved very
" beneficial to the public and the undertakers. Some of
" the first colleries upon its banks are worked out, and
" others have been opened. Its business has been in-
" creased by the large copper-works belonging to the
" Anglesea company erected on one of its branches, and
" by the plate-glass manufactory and other works found-
" ed near it in the neighbourhood of the populous town
" of St. Helen's. On reviewing the present and past
" state of the manufactories and commerce of England,
" the mind is astonished with admiration at the perse-
" vering labour and ingenuity that has atchieved so many
" national and beneficial advantages."

The difficulty of creating an interesting tour by avoid-
ing the sameness attendant on a high road may very
easily be obviated, if the party determined upon an excursion will take the course of any river which may lead
nearest to the place they wish to arrive at, should a river

pass near to such spot. As rivers, and particularly such as are navigable, have generally a number of settlers on their banks, this necessarily requires a passable road, and should there be one on either side of the river, that which is the least frequented is generally the most picturesque; and as canals often accompany rivers, for the purpose of having a ready feeder from the loss they sustain in lockage and drain water, it may usually be taken for granted, there is very seldom a deficiency in scenery of the most beautiful description.

The *Grand Junction* or *Braunston Canal* is so peculiarly distinguished, that truly it may be said, from its junction with the Thames to its termination at Braunston, to be an almost perpetual succession of variegated beauty, shaping its devious course through some of the richest vallies of Middlesex, Hertfordshire, Buckinghamshire and Northamptonshire, accompanied by a redundance of the most luxuriant scenery, and lined on its sides with a succession of rising eminences. It gradually ascends from the bed of the Thames by the means of its locks, the entire way to Marsworth, a distance of nearly forty miles, by the banks of the canal.

At the head of the river Bulburn, between Penley-hill and Marsworth, is its highest level in Hertfordshire, and from the level of the sea, the navigation at this spot is considerably above the top of the cross of St. Paul's.

To make the most interesting tour of the Grand Junction, I should prefer falling in with it at the town of Watford; to which place I would take the route by Paddington, visiting the basin there, and then following the road by Harrow, Stanmore, and over Bushey-heath to Watford.

Paddington, a few years since, was simply a mere high road thoroughfare into Buckinghamshire, and the western parts of Hertfordshire, and was rather celebrated for the nursery and market gardener's grounds in its vicinity. The most celebrated of the former is that belonging to Mr. Jenkins, where an immense stock and tasteful variety of exotics and heaths attract repeated visits from the curious, and have rendered this spot a regular promenade for the nobility and gentry.

Paddington was for many years the residence of the late Mr. George Morland, a painter, of considerable eminence for representing rural and domestic scenery. The eagerness with which his works were sought for after his dissolution, caused the picture-dealers of the metropolis to create manufactories for the purpose of multiplying spurious copies from his originals; and to such a pitch at one time had this infamous traffic arrived, as to render it a well-ascertained fact, that from some of his best pictures not less than *thirty copies* had been made, all of which were palmed upon the public as original productions.

Opposite to the dwelling of Morland was the White-lion inn, where the country carters usually refreshed their cattle, and from the windows of his own house he made innumerable sketches of rustic subjects, while stopping, with which he usually embellished his pictures; and as they were particularly appropriate for his purposes, it is more than probable he selected the situation for the facility of procuring such desirable materials.

The Basin of the Canal at Paddington, is a large square sheet of water occupying many acres, with warehouses on either of its sides, and so commodiously sheltered, that goods of every kind, can be shipped or unloaded without the danger of being wetted. This is a most de-

sireable advantage, as the fly-boats from Manchester bring
a variety of fine articles that require every care. Since the
canal has been brought to Paddington, this place has
become an extensive and well frequented market for
cattle, sheep, butter, poultry, &c. A short distance to
the left of Paddington, are the Grand Junction Water-
works, which now partly supply the west end of the
town. Paddington-green was formerly celebrated for
possessing some of the noblest elm trees in Middlesex,
and has a tasteful little church in its centre. From hence
the road leads by the side of the canal, on the right of
which we are brought to a view of the connection of the
Prince Regent's Canal with that of the Grand Junction.
This ramification, which is now in a fair way of being
speedily completed, commences with a lock at the first
bridge, and after passing through a short tunnel, under
the Edgeware road, it enters the Regent's Park, where
it will form an ornamental sheet of water. Passing from
thence in an easterly direction, it crosses the Hampstead
and Highgate roads ; at the former of which places is a
curious engine for weighing the tonnage in the boats which
are to navigate its surface. After passing the Kentish-
town road, the canal enters the grounds of Mr. Agar, at
the back of Pancrass church and Battle bridge, where a
large basin is forming as a depot for articles of consump-
tion, such as coals, &c. which will be found highly convenient for the inhabitants. Running in a parallel line
with Pentonville high road, it enters the grand tunnel
under Islington, in the front of White Conduit House, and
passes out again by an excavation into Mr. Rhodes's
fields, from thence to Hackney, and under the Mile-end
road into the Thames.

Returning to the Grand Junction, which we cross by
the bridge just before mentioned, the scenery at this spot

is a pleasing presage of what may be expected. Having turned our backs upon the metropolis, we find at the commencement of the canal, emerging from the capital, a very beautiful burst of scenery, the Hampstead hills ranging in a picturesque curvature, crowned by wood, and ornamented with their church and villas, passing off in a north-west direction towards Kilburn and Wilsden-green ; the lofty woods of Kensington on the left, lead away to Holland-house, beyond which the country opens for a considerable space, forming another amphitheatre of pictorial beauty, until it reaches Old Oak Common, and the rising knolls beyond Holsden green, where it unites with those hills that pass from the opposite side.

At *Westbourn Village* we pass the tasteful cottage of Mrs. Siddons, and continue to Kensal green, another pretty hamlet. The canal here takes an inclination to the left, and passing by Wormwood Scrubs, (a considerable space of ground, where the life-guards and other cavalry usually exercise,) enters on Old Oak Common. From the bridge at this spot, and over the stream, Harrow on the Hill presents itself to the eye, and terminates the horizon in a very agreeable form. Here we take our leave of the Paddington canal, which ceases to be interesting all the way it courses, until it falls into the Grand Junction. Continuing the high road, we pass Holsden-green and Stone-bridge, where there is a road-side inn, once a very rustic building, and a place often resorted to by the late Morland, in collecting materials for his canvass. I was once highly gratified with an anecdote relating to this place, and as it must come home to every parent, I should as such be induced almost to envy the feelings of the late Mr. Alderman Boydell.

The two sons of that gentleman had been on a fishing excursion on the banks of the Brent, which passes under

this bridge, when by an accident one of the young gentlemen fell into the river and was near being drowned.
By timely assistance he was saved, and taken to this little
inn, at that time kept by a very worthy woman of the
name of Reed, who administered her share of attention
and ·ultimately succeeded in recovering the youth who
had been a short time under water.   In gratitude to the
Almighty Disposer of all things, he ever afterwards made
a visit to this place, on the same day in every succeeding
year, and in thankful remembrance to the good old lady,
this gentleman and his family always held this a day of
recreation in commemoration of the event.   It happened
that the late Mr. Ibbetson, the landscape draftsman, and
myself were sketching about these parts, and wanting
refreshment, chance threw us into this cottage, where to our
gratification, we arrived on one of these occasions in time
to partake of Mr. Boydell's hospitality, to whom we had
both been long known.   The interesting event, and a fine
day, beside a commission to *each of us* from that gentleman,
could not fail to impress the anecdote on our recollection.

From the Stone-bridge, the road passes away to Sudbury common, on the right of which is Wembley Park,
late the seat of R. Page, Esq. and on the left is Hanger's
hill, and the seat of — Willan, Esq. the celebrated stage-
coach proprietor of the Bull and Mouth Inn, in Alders-
gate-street.

-- *Sudbury Common* is a very rural spot over which our
route leads by a gradual ascent to Harrow on the Hill.
On both sides of the road are several mansions and villas
commanding extensive views into Surrey, Berkshire,
Buckinghamshire, and Middlesex.

Harrow on the Hill has a most imposing appearance,
rising to a considerable height above a rich valley. It
commands the surrounding country in all directions.

In addition to every other beauty which it possesses, it
has an abundance of lofty timber on its summit, and well
clothed with wood on its different brows. The view
from the church-yard overlooks an immense valley in a
westerly and south-westerley direction. In the remotest
distance is Windsor Castle. The Manor-house of Harrow
is the seat of Lord Northwick, whose grounds range
along the eastern side of the hill, and are well worthy of
attention ; parties are often made from town to visit these
scenes of rural and classic abode. The school was
founded by John Lyon, a wealthy yeoman of Preston, in
this parish, in the reign of Queen Elizabeth; and to use
the language of our immortal bard, it .

"Has been abused most cursedly."

It was a favourite residence of Henry VIII. who ex-
changed other lands with Bishop Cranmer for this manor.
Shortly after Henry had taken up his abode here, some
wiseacre predicted that London would be destroyed by a
deluge ; the consequence was, his believers, who were
abundant, flocked to this hill for protection, until the
period of his prediction had passed away.

Descending Harrow Hill to the northward, we come in
view of Mr. Drummond's mansion, and Bentley Priory,
the seat of the late Marquis of Abercorn, built from the
design of John Soane, Esq. R.A.* Leaving Harrow
Weald Common to our left, we enter Great Stanmore, a
pleasant village which skirts the brow of a steep hill for
nearly a mile.

The attention of the traveller is particularly arrested
by a newly erected and picturesque building, on the right
of the road as you ascend from London, nearly on the

* For a minute detail and particulars of these two mansions, see the
Author's work entitled " Rides and Walks thirty miles round London."

middle of the hill, looking towards the south-east, and well defended from the north and north-east. It is a cottage built for Dr. Hooper, under the direction of Mr. Sanderson, in the style of gothic architecture adopted in this country, in the early part of the reign of Henry VIII.

Its general plan appears to be admirably well suited to the situation; it exhibits from the road an entrance front, with an extensive range of offices and stabling, which together form nearly the shape of a horse-shoe. In this arrangement, and the varied parts and outline, the architect has produced a very attractive effect, but a stranger, on viewing this front, might, from its sombre appearance not expect the light and airy structure, and handsome suit of apartments into which he is gradually introduced, forming the south and east fronts, commanding exceedingly beautiful and extensive views of the country.

These apartments open to rustic collonades, and are terminated at the south-west end by a spacious conservatory, decorated in the same style of architecture as the exterior. Convenience and comfort have been the primary considerations in this design; and when time shall have harmonised the tints of the building, and matured the ivy, the woodbine, and the numerous shrubs which are now in their infancy, Stanmore cottage will present a picture of rural beauty not to be equalled within a considerable distance of the metropolis.

Stanmore church, which was built at the sole expense of Sir J. Wolstenholme, Knt., is a brick building, the tower of which is covered with ivy. There is an excellent inn here, built at the expense of the late marquis of Abercorn, and which has his coat of arms as a sign; here is also a celebrated brewery the property of Mr. Clutterbuck.

At the top of Stanmore hill we enter on Bushy heath, and at some distance on the right in the valley catch a

·view of the celebrated reservoir, the property of the Grand Junction Company, on Aldenham common, at the foot of the village of Elstree. This noble sheet of water occupies a space of considerable extent on the verge of Aldenham common, which thirty years ago was a barren waste; here the improvements in agriculture are indeed conspicuous, for at this place a poor, sandy, meagre, wretched soil has now by good husbandry been converted into rich pasturage.

The reservoir has all the appearance of a lake; and when the timber that surrounds it shall have arrived at maturity, it will be a most delightful spot. From this immense sheet of water, in event of drought or a deficiency of upland waters, the lower parts of the Grand Junction and the Paddington canals can have an immediate supply. The feeder from this reservoir enters the main stream near Rickmansworth, above Batchworth mills, and supplies the millers below with 300 locks of water, to whose interest the Duke of Northumberland is a perpetual trustee.

The village of Elstree, surrounded with an abundance of wood is a charming back ground to the reservoir-lake, from the centre of which the church-spire is seen rising among the wood at the summit of its brow. More to the northward, the scenery opens in a broad expanse, and presents the distances towards St. Alban's.

On a large scale this scene would form an excellent subject for the pencil, but the limits of our publication will allow us only to introduce the head of the reservoir, and its accompaniments. Having chosen the latter part of the season for our present route, a period when the cattle-fairs take place in the neighbourhood of the metropolis, we met innumerable droves of beasts at this spot, passing for Barnet and Harlow-bush markets. These

are accompaniments to the picturesque as well as their
drivers, and here we saw them in their natural simplicity;
numbers of them had taken to the lake to lave their heated
limbs and slake their thirst; the drovers, some mounted
and others on foot, were forcing them forward, while
the interest of the scene was heightened by a fresh succession of cattle following up the former droves, enveloped
in all the pictorial effect of clouds of dust strongly tinged
with the diversified rays of the setting sun.

The habiliments of the peasants who attend them are
very picturesque; coming from the interior of Wales,
they usually bring a sort of wardrobe at their backs,
which with long sticks, ragged dogs, and rough ponies,
make up an interesting whole for the artist.

With the decline of the day we hastened through Aldenham, which is a rural and pleasant village, by Otters-
pool and the banks of the Coln to Bushy Mill, and entered Watford in sufficient time for an evening's ramble
through Cashiobury Park, the seat of the Earl of Essex.

Elstree stands upon the old Roman road called the
Watling-street, which here makes an angle at Brockley
hill, passing southward through Edgware to Paddington,
by Tyburn, where it crossed the other Roman road,
called Old-street, (now named Oxford-road,) which
proceeded by the back of Kensington, and through an
unfrequented path, until it fell into the present great
road to Brentford, Staines, &c.

Dr. Stukeley quotes Higden, taking notice that the
Watling-street ran to the west of Westminster, over the
Thames, so through the middle of Kent; hence it is evident it passed through Hyde park and by May fair,
through St. James's park to the street by Old Palace
yard, called the *wool-staple*, to the Thames.

Here has been an old gate, one part of the arch is still

left, but not Roman ; on the opposite side of the river is
Stane-gate ferry, which was the regular continuation of
this street to Canterbury, and so to the three famous sea-
ports, Rutupic, Dubris, and Lemanis.   The Old-street,
now called Oxford-road, was originally carried north of
London, in order to pass into Essex, because London
was then not considerable, but in a little time became well
nigh lost, and Holborn was struck out from it, as con-
ducting travellers thither, directly entering the city at
Newgate, originally called Chamberlain's-gate, and so
to London-stone, (the Lapis Milliaris,) from whence distances were reckoned; and hence the reason why Watling-street is still preserved in the city, though the real
Watling-street goes through no part of it.   The other direction of the Watling street from Elstree passes in a
northerly direction through Radlet, Colney-street, and
St. Albans, and thence to Dunstable and Fenny Stratford,
where we shall again have occasion to notice this celebrated Roman causeway.

WATFORD,

The ancient residence of the renowned British general
Cassibelin, Casibellan, or Cassivellan, is particularly
noticed by Stukely and Baxter, who insist on his private
residence being but a short distance from the city of
Suellaniacis, which was beyond a doubt placed at
Elstree, between Penny-well and Brockley-hill.

Cambden was of opinion that Cashiobury or Casho-
bury was the identical spot where Cassibelin, the King
of the Cassii resided, and that placed from its elevated
situation was very likely to become the head quarters of

a general commanding an army. From the elevation of Cashioberry the surrounding country may be viewed in a southern and western direction, so that any attempt of the Roman army to leave the Watling-street, to surprise the flank of the British army, by passing up the valley between the high ridge of land called Bushy-heath, and Oxey-woods, or by a still more circuitous route of continuing to Rickmansworth, and then debouching from the valley that leads from that town, upon Watford, would readily be perceived and easily frustrated.

. Watford is fifteen miles from London, and is situated on a smart eminence, gradually rising, and terminating with the end of the town. Antiquaries differ very much respecting the etymology of Watford, some considering it Wetford, from its being situated near marshy grounds; others Watling-ford, from its contiguity to Watling-street. It is said also to have been the residence of the Merican kings during the Saxon Heptarchy, till Offa gave it to the Monastery of St. Albans. Of late years it has become a place of considerable traffic and thoroughfare.

Thirty years since, not more than two stage coaches passed through it, but now it is perpetually travelled as a high western road.

The Church is a spacious building, dedicated to the Virgin Mary, and consists of a nave, aisles, and chancel, with a tower at the west end, terminated by a small spire. The chancel, which appears of a more recent date than the nave, opens from the latter by a large pointed arch. On the north side of the chancel is the cemetery of the Morisons, (now of the Essex family,) where are two fine monuments of the family, by Nicholas Stone, who, in his day, appears to have been a man of uncommon talent: the late Lord Orford has given a little history of this artist. At the south side of the church-yard is a.

free school, with apartments for a master and mistress.
It was founded by Mrs. Elizabeth Fuller, of Watford
Place, in 1704, for forty boys, and twenty girls. A
full length portrait of the foundress is preserved in the
school room. Watford is nearly a mile in length: its
entrance from London is very indifferent, though of late
much improved. It is a populous and busy town, with
a market on Tuesday, for corn, straw, platt, &c. There
are two fairs in the year, one on the Tuesday after
Trinity Sunday, and the other on the 9th of September.
The principal manufactory of this town is throwing of
silk, and the paper mills in its neighbourhood employ
many hands. The river Coln runs through the town,
and has excellent fishing. The best inns here, are the
Essex Arms, and Rose and Crown, posting inns, and the
George.

After the dissolution, this manor was granted by Henry
VIII. to R. Morison, Esq. who was employed in many
state affairs by that sovereign, and died at Strasburgh,
in 1556, and from whom the present earl is descended.
This noble family, from an early period, have alike held
the esteem of succeeding monarchs, and of the people,
one of whose best friends they may be considered, Sir
William Capel, who was Lord Mayor of London, in
1503, was a marked object for plunder, by those atrocious villians, Empson and Dudley, the miscreant
minionsof Henry VII.; he was obliged to pay a fine of
2000l., and some years afterwards, was again called on
for a similar sum, but refusing to submit to this second im-
position, he was imprisoned in the Tower till the King's
death. Arthur, the son of Baron Capel, of Hadham, was,
after the restoration, restored to his family possessions,
and created Viscount Malden and Earl of Essex, by
Charles II., in April 1661; in April 1670, he was

sent Ambassador to Denmark, where he bravely supported the honour of his country, and refused to lower
his colours, though fired on by the governor of Cronin-
berg Castle; for which act the governor was afterwards
compelled to beg pardon on his knees. In 1672, he was
appointed lord lieutenant of Ireland, and, in 1680, made
first commissioner of the treasury. Algernon, his son,
the second Earl, married Mary, daughter of William
Bentinck, Earl of Portland. William, the third Earl,
his successor, died in January, 1743, leaving one son,
(by his second wife, daughter of Wriothesley, Duke of
Bedford,) William Ann Holles, the late Earl, who died
in March, 1799. George, his eldest son and successor,
the present Earl, assumed the name of Coningsby, on
succeeding to the estates of his grand-mother, Frances,
daughter of Thomas, Earl of Coningsby. The intrepid
manner in which the present Earl caused the public right
to be respected, by insisting on a free passage for the
subject through St. James's Street and Pall Mall, on a
court-day, and contesting that point personally, with the
household troops and officer on guard, in the street, and
afterwards with the Secretary of State, in the House of
Peers, will incontestibly prove there has been no dege-
neracy in the blood of this nobleman.

The Earl of Essex's mansion at Cashiobury, is a spacious building, situated on an elevation, in an extensive
park. The house has been much improved by its present noble owner, who has added at the west end of the
building, the external appearance of an ancient hall. The
deception is so complete, that when withinside, you are
naturally led to enquire for the great hall or the chapel,
for either of which it may be taken. It is a long pile
in imitation of Gothic architecture with a number of
pointed turrets, and deep window frames in which are

are double compartments painted with the scriptural subjects of the twelve apostles.

The entrance to the house is by a sort of cloister, embellished with stained glass, from whence you pass to the great cloister, which has some ancient stained glass, illustrative of the history of Joseph, and are rare specimens of that art; here also is a wind dial, some curious ebony chairs, and a valuable clock. The staircase contains a portrait of Garrick, and a Flemish piece. From hence we are conducted to

The *Small Library*, in which are a portrait of the Duke of Gloucester, a bust of Bonaparte, and two pictures of Henry 7th and his Queen, by Holbein.

In the *Winter Drawing Room*, are portraits of Lord Capel, by Lely; Sir A. Loftus, Vandyke; Lord Cork, Lord Coningsby, and Henry the 4th, Lord Abergavenny, and Coningsby, Vandyke; Sir R. Jones, by Kneller; Sir Thomas Coningsby, Vandyke; Countess of Kildare, and a curious portrait of a dwarf; Algernon, Earl of Northumberland, his daughter Elizabeth, with a son and daughter, by Lely; and Algernon second Earl of Essex, in armour, very fine.

The *Crimson Drawing Room*, has an excellent likeness of Bonaparte, by Vernet; a copy from Rembrant, with a landscape; a very charming picture by Wouverman; two views by Canaletti, perfect miniatures, sweetly painted and the smallest oil paintings I ever saw by that master; a sea piece by Vandevelde; a virgin and child, Carlo Maratti.; a monk's head, Carlo Dulci, very capital; a landscape, Gainsborough; and a stable scene, Morland; with three drawings by M. A. Turner, Esq. R.A., two of which are in his very best style. Here is also a charming portrait of the countess of Essex, by Sir Joshua Reynolds.

c

Inner Library.—The late Earl of Essex, by Van Somer; the Dowager Countess of Essex, by Sir J. Reynolds; Lord Capel and family, by Cornelius Jansen; William Earl of Essex and a Lady Russel, with Lord Russel, who was beheaded; a beautiful specimen of the antique, in a Sleeping Child. The table, inkstand, &c. in this room, which are all of ebony, originally belonged to the late King of France.

The Great Library contains some excellent portraits by Sir Peter Lely, of Mrs. Strangeways, Lady Monson, the Earl and Countess of Clarendon, Lord C. Hyde, with others by that master; also the Countess Chesterfield, Lady and Lord Percy, by Vandyke; and a collection of excellent busts of the Dukes of Bedford and Wellington, the Emperor of Russia, Bonaparte, Messrs. Fox and Pitt, &c.; and some of the heads of the Cesars: two portraits of Charles the First and his Queen, are exquisite performances from the pencil of the present Countess of Essex. Beneath these in a frame is a piece of the pall which covered the coffin of that monarch; beside which are portraits of King William, and Earl Coningsby, who gallantly fought by that king's side at the battle of the Boyne.

In the *Best Drawing Room* are four large frames, containing very beautiful miniatures and enamels by the present Countess of Essex; some exquisitely painted china, &c. The furniture, which is of the latest fashion, is superb, and displays superior taste.

The Summer Dining Room, which constitutes the lower apartment of the supposed gothic building, contains the portraits of the present Earl and Countess of Essex, by the late Mr. Hoppner, R. A., the likenesses are striking, and their treatment bold, dignified and elegant. From the picture of the Earl there is a private plate executed in the first manner. I do not recollect to have seen one from the Countess as a whole length, though I have reason to believe that in Mr. Hoppner's Collection of British Beauties this portrait of her ladyship was given. Here are also portraits of Algernon Sidney, Earl of Essex, by Vandyke; also of the widow of the Earl of Essex, who was murdered in the Tower, and one of Sir C. Williams, besides Algernon Percy, Lord High Admiral, by Vandyke; and a Lady Morrison, from whom the present earl is descended.

The State Bed Room is decorated with blue and white furniture, and hung with Gobelin tapestry, displaying a village feast, from Teniers, the subject that of making wine, &c. The roof of this apartment is painted azure, and the upper part gilt, with a coronet. In King Charles's room is a full length of Charles I. by Vandyke; Charles II. by Lely, and two female portraits by the same artist.

CASHIOBERRY PARK,

Is where we first fall in with the Grand Junction Canal. Ready permission was granted by the present Earl of Clarendon, and the late Earl of Essex, to allow this great national undertaking to pass through their respective parks; and when we find the opposition that the late Duke of Bridgewater was continually receiving, from parties, through whose premises he was unavoidably often obliged to pass his navigable canals, it must stand as a monumental record, and example, of the urbanity and *amor patriæ*, these distinguished noblemen exhibited for the weal of their country.

Cashioberry Park is entered by a gate at the lodge, a short distance from Watford ; and is to its inhabitants as great a luxury as the parks of Windsor are to the residents of that town. The lodge at this entrance is a tasteful display of what the visitor may expect to meet with in the other parts of the park ; it is an octagon building of one story high, with a profusion of ivy, honeysuckles and roses covering its top and sides, while its back is embowered among lofty trees. From this entrance both a path and carriage road lead to the mansion, which stands on an elevated part of the park, overlooking the opposite scenery in a southern and western direction, and from whence Moor Park is conspicuously grand. Nearly in the front of the entrance to the great house ; is the carpenter's cottage, which is partly embowered in trees, with a vine over its front and to its very summit, interwoven with other flowering shrubs and creepers, with a still greater profusion of roses, lillies and flowers of every description than that at the lodge gate has.

From this spot, we take an immediate south-west direction across the park to the shepherd's residence, which forms an opening to the road on the south side, and is called Thorn Cottage. This habitation is a mixture of the Swiss and English style of cottage building, and like the carpenter's residence has its sweet and blooming accompaniments. It is peculiarly well adapted for a herdsman's retreat, as the cattle can be received in, and out of the park ; without annoying the company passing along the high road to the lodge. The inconvenience of meeting sheep, is too well known to every traveller to need a comment.

From this rural habitation we emerge from a grove in which it stands, in a north-west direction down to a shrubbery which lies at the lowest part of the hill. Here

we pass over what is termed a deer-stile, going up a sort
of step-ladder, and enter the shrubbery, where a rustica-
ted and monastic-like gate, with a bell placed at its top,
opposes the entrance into the garden of the Swiss cottage.
The costume of the Swiss country is represented here in
all its minutiæ. On opening the door an immediate view
is had of the cottage; you ascend the gallery around the
building, by a flight of steps from the garden, the usual
method adopted in that country, instead of rising to the
upper story by an internal staircase. The lower apartments consist of a neat little dining room, fitted up in a
rural manner, with stained glass windows exhibiting the
manners and costume of Switzerland, with some Swiss
views, and a curious collection of different specimens of
foreign china; the chairs, &c. are all correspondent.
This tasteful apartment is where parties who have permission from the noble owner, are allowed to take their
dinner or any other refreshment they may chuse to carry
with them. The persons who inhabit the Swiss cottage,
consist of his Lordship's groom and family. The wife of
this domestic provides culinary utensils and all the appa-
ratus requisite for the comfort and accommodation of
those who visit this charming place. At the northern
extremity of the cottage on the first floor, is another room
of a similar description, for accommodation in the event
of two parties visiting at the same period. The other rooms
are appropriated to the use of the regular inhabitants of the
cottage. In the front of the dining room is a small lawn,
and on either side an abundant shrubbery, whilst a bold
and rapid stream emerges from the recesses of a wood on
the right, and passes by the end of the lawn in view of
the house.

Towards the extremity of the grounds on the left, a

rustic bridge is thrown over the river, which answers the double purposes of a weir and dam.

Crossing the bridge, we leave this fairy-ground by a path, through the opposite wood, to his lordship's fisherman's cottage, another pretty retreat most pleasantly situated on the banks of the Grand Junction Canal, and an excellent station for checking the depredations of the boatmen, who navigate the vessels on that stream. This cottage has also its rural embellishments, but differs in its form, being a square building with a slate roof. On the left we pass over a wooden bridge, and enter the park on the right; from hence we continue along the towing path, until we reach another bridge, which connects both sides of the park together. On the right at this place, the bed of the river Gade forms a large sheet of water, over which there is also a bridge ; on the opposite side is the mill, and a waterfall, occasioned by the superfluous or waste water beyond what the mill requires. The scenery here is very picturesque, having an abundance of wood, embowering the mill and cascade, which are continually enlivened, by the herds of cattle and deer, which usually prefer passing through the shallow water, to the road by the bridge.

A gravel road beyond this on the left, lined on either side with trees, leads up the hill to the miller's residence the fourth cottage in the park. At a short distance on this brow of the hill, a seat is placed under the boughs of a wide spreading oak, from whence we have the best view of Cashioberry great house and grounds. The miller's cottage is situated at another extremity of the park, embowered in wood, with a small opening on the right: except the south front of this cottage the whole is overgrown with ivy, and presents a most beautiful *coup d' oeil.* The carriage way still continues through grounds that belong to the estate, until it reaches the lane which divides the parks of the Earls of Essex and Clarendon.

At this termination of the Cashioberry woods, stands another beautiful cottage, inhabited by one of his lordship's keepers, and called by the country people *Sparrow pot lodge.*

There is another route through the park, by keeping along the banks of the Grand Junction until you reach Grove Mill bridge.

After leaving the mill stream in the park we passed a lock of the navigation into which a pair of boats were just entering : the busy scenes during the process of passing the locks; form excellent incidents for the landscape painter.

About a short half mile from hence, brings us to a watchman's cottage belonging to the Canal Company, whose occupation is partly to prevent the navigators from committing depredations in their passage through the park; for which purpose a vista is cut through the plantations, so that a view of the boats may be distinctly had, during their passing from hence to the fisherman's cottage at the opposite extremity of the park, and *vice versa.*

This dwelling resembles those erected by the Earl of Essex, and has innumerable flowers and flowering shrubs surrounding it. Here again is another lock on the canal.

Prior to the boats entering a lock, they carry the horses which draw their respective loads forward, and in this interval they feed from a small bottle of hay which is suspended from the side of their collar. Both boats having entered abreast of each other, the water on this side of the lock being at the lowest level, the boy in attendance shuts the flood-gates behind the boats, so that they appear at the bottom of a long square tank. The attendant on land then takes an iron crow, with which, by easy pur-

chase, he raises up a flood-gate, when the water rushes
with an impetuosity into the basin of the lock, and
raises the boats to the upper level in about six minutes.
As soon as the water has thus found its proper level, the
boy instantly opens the opposite gate, andthe barges pass
away, leaving the high water gates open, boats perhaps
being in sight and wanting to go down the stream. The
whole time from opening the first gate to rising into the
upper stream, occupies at this place about seven minutes.
In the locks higher up, towards Stoke Bruern and about
Braunston, the boats do not take up more than three minutes in their passage.

Just before reaching this cottage, the river Gade is
seen entering the navigation from a grove of trees, by
passing under a wooden bridge on the left, where the
park continues on the same side of the stream until it
reaches behind Grove Mill, a remarkable pleasant situation.

Opposite Grove Mill, the Park turns up to the right of
Grove Lane, where we visited the cottage of Lady
Monson, a sister of this noble family, whose delightful
residence is a still further exhibition of the taste of the
earl of Essex. The simplicity exhibited on the outside
of this cottage is finely contrasted by a corresponding
elegance within. The paintings of her ladyship's daughter, which embellish many parts of the ornamental furniture, exhibit no small degree of ability. From this Pa-
radise in miniature, we pass by a path through the
garden, up the hill, to another cottage built very much
in the manner of the Swiss, and roofed with thatch.

This habitation, which is denominated Turf Cottage,
is occupied by Miss Madison, and may be classed as a
cottage orneé. From these fairy places we return by a
gravel walk through the park where is seen on the right

in a valley, enclosed on three sides by a plantation and
some noble timber, the park and head game-keepers'
residence, which is a cottage somewhat in the French
style of building, with a projecting portico.

At this keepers' lodge there is a division of the park,
the part we had just past, being appropriated to a preserve
for pheasants and hares, while the other parts constitute
the deer park. The gardens which belong to Cashioberry are on the left; and no care or expence has been
spared, to place them in the first rank of excellence. A
walk of a mile and a half from Lady Monson's cottage,
brought us again in front of Cashioberry House, after a
ramble of five miles.

The Grand Junction Canal, after leaving the Earl of
Essex's domain, immediately enters the premises of the
Earl of Clarendon, at Grove Mill: here the overshot
waste of water forms a picturesque fall. In places
where the company have not been able, or it has not
been convenient for the residents to have a stone arched
·bridge, they have thrown across the navigation stream,
swing bridges; which are readily passed by the craft,
and prevent a heavy drag for the horses that are employed
at the mill. The scenery that surrounds the turn of
the water at this spot, is embellished with a quantity of
noble timber, which rising in bold masses, are delightfully reflected on the glassy surface of the stream. In
this remote recess we were highly entertained with the
warbling of two nightingales; the place, the serenity of
the evening, and a delightful walk, had put us in full
possession of our faculties, to enjoy every beauty, that
nature presented either to the sight or ear; object after
object in rich and varied succession enchanted our senses
all the way, as we advanced towards

The GROVE PARK, the seat of the Earl of Clarendon,

whose mansion is an old substantial brick building, situated on a considerable eminence, in the centre of the park, to the left above the river Gade and the navigation, which near Grove mill unite their courses, but are almost immediately again divided by the back water, and that which goes to supply the mill wheels, where the river again forms a fresh bed for its current, and passes as before observed once more into the Grand Junction in Cashioberry park.

The manor of the Grove, was purchased by Thomas Villiers, Earl of Clarendon, who married Lady Charlotte Capel, daughter of William, Earl of Essex, and grandson of the great Earl of Clarendon. The park is of considerable extent, passing in a westerly direction for a considerable distance, towards the back road that leads from Hunton bridge to Rickmansworth. In the park are two elegant buildings, viz. the Ionic temple, an edifice merely of ornament, and not intended for any particular use ; the other was taken, as to its proportions, which are correct according to the rules of architecture, from a building called the Temple of Pan, in the grounds of South Lodge, built by the celebrated Lord Chatham, on Enfield Chase. This is something in the rustic style, as being more correspondent with the scenery.

The gardens belonging to this mansion, are on a gentle brow to the northward, and the approach to the house from the Watford road, is by a carriage-way from the lodges at its entrance, over a handsome stone bridge, which is thrown across the navigation, and passes a ford of the river Gade up to the house. The inside contains a most excellent collection of pictures, principally portraits brought from Cornbury, in Oxfordshire ; amongst which we have selected the following :—

In the *Hall*, are portraits of Francis, Lord Cottington ;

the Earl of Kinnoul, Vandyke; Queen of Bohemia, Jansen; William, Marquis Hertford, Vandyke; the Earl of Portland; Queen Elizabeth; James I.; Lord Burleigh; his son, the first Lord Salisbury; Lord Chancellor Clarendon; and the Earls of Jersey and Rochester.

In the *Saloon*, are portraits of a Dutchess and her daughters; Queens Mary and Anne; William III.; James II.; Lord Chancellor Clarendon; Henry Earl of Clarendon; Earl of Rochester and Lady; Lady Charlotte Hyde; Dutchess of Queensberry; Jane, Countess of Essex; Queen Catharine of Portugal; and two excellent pictures of a bull and a horse, the property of Lord Clarendon, by Stubbs.

Drawing Room.—The Countess of Clarendon, second wife of the Lord Chancellor, and her father and mother, Sir Thomas and Lady Aylesbury, by Vandyke; James Stuart, Duke of Richmond, who offered to be a vicarious victim for Charles I.; Mary Dutchess of Beaufort; Thomas Earl of Arundel, Vandyke; Lady Newport; Sir Henry Capel Waller, the poet; Sir Geoffrey Palmer; and the Lord Keeper Coventry, by Jansen.

Dining Room.—Villiers, Viscount Grandison, Vandyke; George Villiers, Duke of Buckingham; William and Philip, Earls of Pembroke; Lord and Lady Cornbury; Lady D'Aubigny; Count de Borgne; Earl and Countess Derby; Sir John Minors; and Lord Goring, all by Vandyke; Lady Barbara Villiers; and Phillip Villiers, Grand Prior of France, 1521.

Staircase.—The Duke of Saxony, and the reformers Selden and Spelman; and in the library is a portrait of the Duke of Monmouth.

I would recommend to parties who make their visits to the two parks of the Earls of Clarendon and Essex, to have their horses taken forward to the village at Hunton

bridge, there to await their arrival ; or else if they should
make distinct visits to the two parks, to alight at the
bottom of Grove lane, and then have them conveyed to
Hunton bridge, as the walk after leaving Grove Park is
remarkably pleasant, the whole way being by the banks of
the navigation ; or perhaps it might be more agreeable to
visit them from Watford, while the refreshment of a party
is preparing at that place.   Hunton Bridge is a pleasant
village, situated on the Gade and the Grand Junction, and
has many very picturesque objects in its vicinity. Langleybury, the mansion of the Rev. Sir John Filmer, Bart.
which is seen to advantage on our left, originally formed
part of the estate of the monastery of St. Albans, and
came to the crown upon its dissolution.   Soon afterwards
it was granted to Sir R. Lee ; from him to the Childs' family, and again to Sir Robert Raymond, from whom it
descended into the Filmer family.   The present proprietor, Sir John Filmer, Bart. is the seventh baronet of the
family.

   Langleybury, which is situated on a rising ground,
from its back front, commands a view of the valley to
the south, while the principal front of the house takes
all the vale of King's Langley in a bird's-eye view below
it.   The same burst of scenery is observable from the
first field beyond Hunton bridge ; where the river and
the canal meander in a variety of serpentine directions,
until reaching the lock at the foot of King's Langley,
where the lowest part of the valley, is closed up with tall
timber, the hills and woods that are above and accompany the scene, extend for a considerable distance towards
the horizon.   The road to this village has a gentle elevation all the way from Hunton Bridge, and forebodes a
continuance of delightful scenery. The valley, though
confined, is cheerful and luxuriant, highly cultivated in

The Vale of Kings' Langley.

Drawn by J. Hassell

all its parts, and presents either a redundance of corn or fertile pasturage: little more than a mile brought us to King's Langley. At the entrance of this village on the right is its parish church, at once a picturesque and remarkable object, giving a character to the view, seen in any direction it may be; but particularly from Hunton Bridge. Within this church are memorials of Sir John Verney; Prince Edmund of Langley, was here born and buried, one of the sons of Edward III. and his wife Isabel, daughter of Pedro King of Castile; there is also a tomb of Piers Gaveston, the favourite of Edward II. King's Langley derives its name from a palace built by Henry III.: a very small corner of the ruins is still to be seen. Richard II. was buried here, but afterwards removed to Westminster, by order of Henry V. The palace, park and manor were given by James I. to Henry Prince of Wales. The Earl of Essex is now lord of the manor.

Passing down the lane by the side of the church, we visited the lock, where the fall of the lock water is very considerable. The scenery from the bridge is so extremely interesting, that we were induced to make a sketch of it. The back water part is particularly picturesque, appearing like the junction of two rivers: it becomes an excellent accompaniment, and communicates a most agreeable variety to the scene.

Continuing for a short distance along the lower lane, we pass the overshot back-water of Langley mill, and enter again upon the high road, which still continues skirting the brow of the western hills that encompass the valley. Rather more than a mile onward is a newly erected mansion, the seat of Mr. Dickinson, of the firm of Longman and Dickinson.

At a short distance beyond this, we see the navigation

making a deviation in the valley, exhibiting a succession
of bridges and locks, passage boats, with horses and their
drivers in different directions, having noble back grounds
and a profusion of wood, forming altogether, abundant
incidents for the pencil of the artist.

Apsley paper Mills, also the property of Messrs. Longman and Dickinson, are the next objects of notice; these
within a short period have been considerably enlarged, occupying a large space of ground, and rather resembling a
village than a manufactory. That most ingenious in-
vention, the manufacturing of paper, was first introduced
into this country by a German. Such of our readers who
never may have seen the process of manufacturing this
useful article, will be highly gratified in visiting a paper
mill. The machinery of this mill is entirely worked by
steam, from the washing of rags to the keeping the pulp
in a state of motion, while taken into the mould, from
whence it is placed between flannels until it sets; and
afterwards it is pressed, dried and sorted for the market.

A short mile brings the canal to an open country, at
Two Waters. On a pleasant brow to the right, overlooking the vale in every direction, is the villa of Mrs. White,
and farther on, near the bridge, are the paper mills of Mr.
Nichols. It was at these mills, that Messrs. Fourdinier
procured a patent for manufacturing paper to any length;
from which circumstance the antiquaries, and water-
colour draftsmen, have derived the advantage of making
their drawings of any dimensions, which was formerly a
very serious inconvenience, from seams unavoidably being
made in the centre of their designs.

At Two Waters the valley expands considerably, taking
a double direction; that on the right leads to Hemel
Hempstead and Gaddesdon, from whence the river Gade
issues, and joins the Bulborn, and the Grand Junction;

Kings Langley Lord... Herts

which afterwards continues by the name of the Gade. The spire of Hempstead church, is seen rising amidst the richly wooded scenery that surrounds it. Our return being through that town, we shall give a more particular account of it hereafter.

. To the left we course the beautiful valley of Box Moor, which presents a profusion of rural scenery; some exqui- site pictures have of late years been exhibited at the Royal Academy, from studies made at this spot Innu- merable groupes of cattle are seen wandering in all parts of the valley, with sheep and horses in every direction.

The scenery at Box Moor is most beautiful on a fine morning. The objects require a prominent effect, and as the sun rises from behind the eastern hills, it lights up the valley with peculiar splendour. There are some scenes which require massing, others again want detaching, to give them an interest, which I consider to be the case here.

. At two miles the moor compresses, and leads between some closing hills, by the village of Broad Way to Bourn end; from Two Waters, on the opposite side of the Grand Junction, rise the hills of Crouch-field, Green-end, and Pinkwell, with scattered cottages on their brows, and a lock house on the canal. Beyond Bourn End, we have little interesting until we reach Berkhamstead; at the entrance of this town is the elegant seat of Mr. Pechell, opposite to whose mansion is Mr. Moore's house, plea- santly situated on the banks of the stream.

BERKHAMSTEAD,

Called originally Berghamstead or Berkhamstead, and
according to Norden, in the Saxon time, Berghamstedt,
because it was surrounded by hills. Berg, signifies a
hill, ham, a town, and stedt, a seat. It was at Berkhamstead that Frederick, Abbot of St. Albans, impeded the
march of William I., by causing the trees on the road
side to be felled, and laid across the way.

Dr. Stukeley affirms this place to have been a Roman
station, and other antiquarians state it to have been *Du-*
rocobrivis. Berkhamstead castle has been a royal possession since the conquest, at which period it constituted
part of the domain of the Earl of Montaigne, the brother-
in-law of William. It was given by Edward III. to the
Black Prince, together with the Dukedom of Cornwall.
It has since descended from the crown to the successive
Princes of Wales, and is at present held under lease of
His Royal Highness the Prince Regent. There anciently
belonged to Berkhamstead lordship fifty towns and
hamlets in the counties of Herts, Bucks, and Northampton, and the tenants were accustomed to do service at
this town, which has of late years been relaxed; the
courts being now held in each county, and the tenants
pay a pecuniary consideration to be excused the above
service. Berkhamstead formerly sent members to parliament, and it was incorporated by James I., whose
children were nursed here, at Berkhamstead-place, an
agreeable situation on a considerable hill, at the extremity of the town,-to the right; during the war between
Charles I. and the Parliament, this corporation sunk into
oblivion. The church of St. Peter is a noble pile of

gothic architecture, with eleven apostles on its pillars, with each of them a sentence of the creed; and on the twelfth pillar is St. George killing the dragon. St. John's chapel, in the church, is used as a school. Berkhamstead gives the title of Marquis to the Duke of Cumberland, and is famous for bowl-turning, shovel and spoon manufacturing, and lace-making.

The free-school here is a strong brick edifice, situated at the bottom of the church-yard; it was founded principally through the exertions of Dr. Incent, dean of St. Paul's during the reign of Henry VIII; who granted, as an endowment to it, the possessions of the fraternity of St. John the Baptist. It received further endowments in the following reign, being incorporated as a royal foundation by the title of " The master, chaplain, and usher of the free school and chantry of Dean Incent, of Berkhamstead." The master has a handsome salary, and apartments at one end of the school-house, the right of appointment belongs to the king; the centre of the building is occupied by the school-room, and the other end by the apartments belonging to the chaplain and usher; the number of boys admitted upon the foundation is 144, it being required that all such are lawfully subjects of the king, and not the children of aliens; the building of this school-house occupied 20 years.

Besides the school just mentioned, there is another, supported by voluntary contributions among the parishioners.

There is also an alms-house endowed with 50l. per ann. for the relief of six poor widows; this was further enriched by the bequest of John Sayer, Esq. in the year 1681.

To give an adequate idea of this town and castle, we shall give Dr. Stukeley's words:—

D

" From Dunstable the Itinerary leads us out of the
" road, going straight to Verolam, and takes in another
" station by the way, *Durocobrivis;* which demonstrates
" it was made not so much for travellers, as for the sol-
" diery or officers who were to visit the garrisons, therefore
" comprehends as many as could conveniently be taken
" into that route. About this station antiquaries have
" been much divided, when it certainly ought to be placed
" at *Berghamsted,* commonly *Barkamstead,* in *Hertford-*
" *shire,* which well suits the assigned distances from
" *Magiovinium,* and the subsequent *Verolanium,* and
" has evidently been a *Roman* town, as its name imports,
" and probably the castle there stands upon a *Roman*
" foundation. 'Tis certain *Roman* coyns are frequently
" dug up there. The inside within the walls, where the
" lodgings were, is about two acres; the entrance was
" not at the corner where now, but in the front of the
" south side. Many chimnies remain in the wall of the
" lodgings, which extended quite round, leaving a spa-
" cious court within, and all the windows looked inward.
" The ground of the court is distinguishable, being good
" soil, and there they find the *Roman* coyns, the rest is
" rubbish and foundations; so that the Saxon castle was
" made upon the Roman. The chapel seems to have
" stood against the west wall, where be signs of a stair-
" case; the walls are of flints gathered from the high
" lands, very thick and laid with strong mortar. This
" town fully answers the distance in the Itinerary, and
" remarkably the import of the name, according to Mr.
" Baxter's derivation, though he erroneously places it at
" *Woburn,* civitas paludosi profluentis; for here is a large
" marsh or bog, wherein the ancient British oppidum was
" placed. 'Tis most sweetly surrounded with high, hard,
" and pleasant ground all around, full of hedge-rows,

" pastures and arable.   The castle was set very judici-
" ously in the north side, upon a piece of dry ground,
" encompassed with springs, by the Saxons made exceed-
" ingly strong.   The town is on the south side of the
" marsh, stretching itself a good length in handsome
" buildings and a broad street ; the church is a handsome
" building, full of chapels and monuments, old and new."

With respect to what Berkhamstead church might
have been, and continued in Dr. Stukeley's time, we have
his authority for, but 'what it is now is another thing.
During the repairs of this building in September, 1818,
we visited it, and found the remorseless hands of churchwardens and overseers stripping the walls of their relics,
and causing a general mutilation of its antiquities.   That
abominable mania, called beautifying and repairing, may
generally be considered as illustrative of the acts of modern Goths and Vandals, destroying the richest works of
past times, and substituting a daubing of whitewash to
hide their barbarism.

There are two modern monuments, by Bacon, over a
vault in a chapel belonging to the church, with the following inscription ;—

" *Faculty;* making a burial vault for John Dorrien,
" Esq. and his family for ever, exclusive of all persons, at
" or in the north chancel of the parish church of Berk-
" hamstead, St. Peter, 12 feet in length, 8 in breadth,
" and 7 feet in depth.   Dated Hitchen, 15th Nov. 1802.
" Signed, Richard Tristram, deputy register.   Sealed
" with the office seal."

On each side of the above notification, are placed the
two monuments, one to the memory of John Dorrien,
Esq. who died in the year 1784, aged 78 years, with the
figure of Hope reclining ; the other, an emblem of Faith,
is to the memory of Ann, relict of the said J. Dorrien,.

Esq. who died Anno Dom. 1802, aged 73 years. There
are also monuments to the Torrington family, with brasses
affixed to them of Richard Torrington and Margaret
his wife.   Berkhamstead castle has a double garden
within its walls, one part of which is appropriated to the
use of its proprietor, the Earl of Bridgewater's establishment at Ashridge ; the other part is for the benefit of the
inhabitant and his family, who is a game-keeper, and occupies the cottage at its entrance.   Its outside is a continued circumference of dilapidated walls, over which the
ivy, which once contributed to its decay, now partly
supports it, binding with its stems and integuments large
masses of the building.   There are plenty of excellent
springs at its entrance, and one in particular, of uncom-
monly sweet water, behind the first cottage in the
grounds.   The ground on the outside of the wall is appropriated to a rabbit warren, which is abundantly stocked.
    The town of Berkhamstead has a very picturesque
appearance, viewed from near the entrance of the castle,
where the navigation and the Bulborne, traversing the
valley, add considerable interest to the scene.
    The Grand Junction, on leaving Berkhamstead, con-
tinues its course under the hills, cloathed with a profusion of woods, and at a mile distant passes the valley,
at the back of St. Mary's North church, a pleasant rural
village, with two gentlemen's residences ; that on the right
is occupied by Major Moor, the other, on the left, by the
Rev. Mr. Drake.   We leave Hill Green on the left, and
soon gain a view of Dudswell and Northcourt on the
opposite hills, and speedily reach a respectable little inn
and farm, called the Cow Roast.
    This spot I should conceive, to be most erroneously
named. It is famed for the richest pasturage. The
meadows on the sides of the Grand Junction are luxu-

riant in the extreme, and during the dreadful drought in August of last year, 1818, the whole of the Cow Roast valley was in a state of the most fertile vegetation. Here we saw herds of cows grazing, and observed a fresh drove of sucklers with their calves coming up to remain for the night, and we found, upon enquiry, that this inn was one of the regular stations for the drovers halting their cattle for refreshment; hence I should suppose, the proper name is the *Cow Rest*, or resting place of those animals, for along the road, and all the way through, the breeding and grazing parts of Bucks, Bedfordshire, and Northampton-shire, there is a perpetual supply of cows passing to the capital, which forms a profitable trade to the farmers and graziers of those counties.

On the right of the road at the Cow-roast, a lane leads to the navigation, at the distance of about an hundred yards; there are two cottages on the banks of the canal, which are called the *Water-guage* houses, one of which is inhabited by a servant of the Grand Junction Company, the other is occupied by a person placed there by the Duke of Northumberland.

Both of these persons keep an accurate account of the height of water at all hours of the day, and also at the times of the different boats passing the locks.

A deficiency of what is termed the river stream, or back-water, for supplying the bed of the river Bulbourn, which turns the wheels of the paper-mills upon that river, occasioned a protracted litigation between the Company and Messrs. Longman and Dickinson, who ultimately obtained damages against the Company.

The right, with respect to the property of the water of a river passing with a navigable cut, is not always accu-rately understood; for occasionally the river is entirely thrown into the cut: but where the property of mill-stream was exercised prior to the making of the navigation, the projectors of the navigation have been compelled to throw off the canal, an adequate supply of water for the purposes of such mills, otherwise private property might be violated with impunity.

In a number of instances the canal crosses the beds of the different rivers that supply its deficiency, and having received the necessary quantity for its upland navigation, the supplying river is again thrown into its ancient bed, where it remains undisturbed until wanted for the same purpose again.

This process is very perspicuously illustrated at King's Langley lock, where the water that turns the Langley mills, the back-water cut, to those mills, and the surplus stream-water of the canal, which occasions a sort of cascade at that spot, unite and form a bold current, passing through the valley to Hunton-bridge, where the streams divide, and a similar occurrence takes place again at that village.

It may seem singular for what purpose the Duke of Northumberland should keep a water-gauger at this place. The case is, that the Company want an equal supply of water below from the Duke's property, in return for what they supply above. Thus, if five hundred locks of water are given for the use of the millers, to whom the Duke is trustee, they (the Grand Junction Company) in return receive an equal quantity below; at Cowley lock, near Uxbridge, the Grand Junction have a servant to keep a check of water against the Duke's agent at that place: by this means, and the excellent regulations of the Company's committee, all litigation is avoided, and the millers on the stream know to a certainty what quantity of water they are to depend upon. The cottages at the Cow-roast lock have a picturesque appearance, being white, slated on the roofs, and backed with a plenty of wood.

The sheet of water above the lock makes a sweeping circuit until it reaches a bridge in the distance where the hills, covered with wood, declining gradually towards the level of the canal, closes up the scene. The boats in motion at the opening and shutting of the locks, and the various avocations of the attendants, constitute very appropriate incidents, and form excellent embellishments for landscape.

From hence the canal passes through the opening of the hills of Penley, Northcourt, and Albury, and at the distance of three miles reaches the head of the river Bulbourn, near to which is the source of the Dandel and Thame rivers. We have here another ridiculous tradition of the name of this little river; the etymology of which, according to the country folk, is derived from a bull having been burned at this spot alive. The solution is much more simple, as from an analysis of the very name Bulbourn, it will clearly appear to signify a place or river frequented by that beast; a *bourn*, in the Scottish acceptation implying a rivulet.

The good folks in these parts have originally been proverbial for their credulity and prejudices, a specimen of which we shall have very shortly to relate, in our account of Tring. The horse-road now leaves the valley, and we ascend Penley Hill: on the rise of it to the right, we have an interesting piece of scenery, with Albury and its church tower at the foot of a high down; from thence the view extends towards Pittlesthorn under the Ashbridge hills. Penley-hill is wooded to its summit, from whence, after a steep descent, we enter the town of Tring.

Tring, a small, irregular built market town, is situated at one of the extremities of Hertfordshire, in a north-westerly direction, and is bounded by Buckinghamshire on that side. It has a neat market house, newly erected;

the market is held on a Friday, for the sale of corn, straw for platt, &c.; there is also an annual fair held here, upon the 29th of September. Tring is eight miles from Aylesbury, four from Windover, and thirty-one from London.

During the Saxon heptarchy this town gave name to a hundred, of which it was the capital. The parish church, dedicated to St. Peter and St. Paul, is a spacious and well-proportioned structure, having a large square tower of considerable elevation at its west end, and strengthened by massive buttresses. The interior of the building is divided into a nave, aisles, and chancel. The nave and aisles are separated by six lofty pointed arches, springing from clustered columns of considerable height. The vestry occupies the lower part of the tower, which was originally connected with the nave by an acute arch. The timber frame-work of the roof rests at each side upon supporters, which are terminated by curious devices carved upon them, as a monkey holding a book and purse; Nebuchadnessar, represented with a human face and long beard joined to a lion's body; and other emblems of this kind, productions of the artist's monstrous imagination. Within the church are several monumental tablets affixed to the walls, and the altar-piece is tolerably executed, representing Moses and Aaron, with the two tablets of the commandments.

Tring is distinguished for an atrocious occurrence which took place in the year 1751. Some ignorant country people, alarmed at the mortality produced among their cattle by a contagious disorder then prevalent, attributed all the mischief to the witchcraft of John and Ruth Osborne, an old married couple of this town, and, assembling in a riotous manner, proclaimed their accusation to the public at the three neighbouring market towns of

Winslow, Leighton Buzzard, and Hemel Hempstead, upon their respective market days. The following was the form of the proclamation made at Hemel Hempstead.

"This is to give notice, that on Monday next, a man and woman are to be publicly ducked at Tring in this county, for their crimes."

According to this notice these bigotted and superstitious rioters seized the unfortunate victims of their persecutions, dragged them from the vestry of the church, to which, on account of its sanctity, they had fled as a place of refuge, and ducked them so severely that the old woman, already weighed down almost to the grave by the pressure of years, affliction and infirmities, expired on the spot, and was followed in a very few days by her aged husband. The coroner's verdict declaring that they were wilfully murdered, several of the ring-leaders in this barbarous transaction were brought to trial and capitally convicted.

Here is a charity-school, for the education and clothing of twenty boys, and a Sunday-school has been founded within the last few years, for the instruction of about eighty boys and girls. The manufacture of straw-platt and making of lace, constitutes the chief employment of the inhabitants.

On the south side of the road, adjoining the town of Tring, is Tring Park, the residence of Edmund Yates, Esq.; it is the property of the heirs of the late Sir Drummond Smith, Bart. The park contains three hundred acres of land (part of it not very excellent). The view from the south front of the mansion, is enlivened by a most beautiful hanging wood, which extends itself from the plain to the summit of a very bold hill, along the southern extremity of the park. A way by the side of the wood has been made by the labourers in passing from the home-yard to

the farm beyond the park, which appears rather curious'
by having been indented by the right and left foot alternately. At the extremity of the wood, on a considerable
eminence, is a very tasteful white building, denominated
the summer house, which is occupied by one of Mr.
Yates's domestics. Here is a stone obelisk, twenty feet
high at least, erected on the spot, where several vistas
cut through the wood, intersect each other, and from
whence some very choice scenery is seen. The park is
well stocked with deer, and agreeably diversified with
hill and dale. The dwelling-house is spacious, elegant,
and commodious; it is a modern, white-fronted building,
with a portico at the grand entrance.

We leave Tring by the road to the village of Marsworth, or more properly Meresworth, which is laid down
by Stukeley as its proper name, from possessing a *mere*,
or small lake, which received the waters from the surrounding hills of the Chiltern hundred, which here ter-
minate the northern boundary of Hertfordshire, and passing Tring in a north-westerly direction, again turn more
to the westward, and pass away into the heart of Buckinghamshire.

The other branch of these hills, as before observed,
take an inclination towards Dunstable, rising southward
above the old Roman road, the Icening or Ickneld way,
which now principally constitutes the high road from
Tring to the foregoing town.

On the road to Marsworth, by a bridge, we cross the
navigable feeder, which comes from Windover, and passing the Weston reservoir, joins the Grand Junction at the
head of the river Bulbourn, near which is the residence
of Mr. Lake, the engineer to the Company for these parts
of the canal. A mile before we reach Marsworth, we
traverse the banks of the three celebrated reservoirs of

Marsworth, from the Reservoirs. — Bucks.

Drawn by I. Hassell.

water that belong to the navigation. On our left, which is the lowest of the three, there is a steam engine erected on an eminence above the pool, which has some pretty accompaniments, and forms a lake in miniature. The large reservoir is on the opposite side of the embankment, and lies between the upper and lower reservoirs; it occupies an area of many acres, and is very picturesque: the village and church of Marsworth crown the top of the opposite hill, and are beautiful objects for enlivening the landscape. A view of this scene accompanies our work; indeed the principal scenes about these parts are highly interesting. The upper water is separated from the main body by an embankment, which is made the foot-way to the village before us.

Continuing onwards we descend a steep hill, on the right of which is a sort of coffer-dam to the lake. In boisterous weather these meres have a considerable swell, and break over the dams with fury : when flying clouds occasionally obstruct the gleams of the sun which can only partially break on the lake scenery, the effects are generally grand, and attract the peculiar attention of the artist.

Marsworth, or Meresworth, is pleasantly situated on a brow, overlooking the vale of Aylesbury. This spot has certainly been of some consequence, and though I cannot find any notice taken of it by Camden, Stukeley, or any other antiquarian, I am thoroughly satisfied it has been of considerable importance. Its elevated situation points it out as a key to the different Roman stations among the hills that surround it.

At the back of the church, towards Pittlesthorn and Ivinghoe, there is a considerable rise, from the summit of which you have an extensive view over the open valley of Aylesbury ; from hence the eye commands every avenue or entrance to the Chiltern Hills, from Wendover

to Leighton Buzzard. Mr. Greening, a farmer, who
has been resident in this village upwards of sixty
years, remembers to have seen innumerable articles dug
up here, such as parts of swords, urns, coins, and
pieces of armoury, all of which, from their description,
were evidently Roman; and when the excavation was
making for the bed of the Grand Junction Canal, there
were found a vast quantity of Roman urns, and coins.
Charles Harvey, Esq. M.P. of Great George-street, Westminster, had several of the urns, and some of the
coins presented to him, and they now ornament his
library. The bed of the navigation, passing round
the base of the brow on which the village stands,
might probably, from its appearance, have been an outer
wall of a small station or watch tower, belonging to those
people, for the purpose of giving an alarm in the event
of any irruption from the lower country, by the Britons,
attempting to force a passage through either of the
passes of the Chiltern Hills, towards the metropolis of the
empire, or for the purposes of taking the armies of their
enemies in the rear. My opinion that Marsworth has
been peculiarly distinguished for its remains of antiquity,
is considerably strengthened from examining the premises
of Mr. Horner, at the lower part of the hill, and the appearances at the vicarage-house nearly opposite.

In Camden's Brittania, of Buckinghamshire, anno
1730, he describes Marsworth, a vicarage in the hundred
of Cotslow and deanery of Muresley, and the valuation
9l. 9s. 5d.; in the patronage of Trinity College, Cambridge, and the then incumbent Mr. John Theed. This
vicarage house is surrounded by a moat of deep water,
the walls of brick work, are very little impaired by
time, and bear all the external appearance of having been
a monastic establishment. Opposite the old abbey now

Mr. Horner's house, there is a square plot of ground
converted into an orchard of about an acre, surrounded
with another moat, much broader than at the vicarage,
and considerably deeper; the interior of the area of this
ground is lower than the embankment towards the moat,
and has great inequalities on its surface.   On enquiry of
Mr. Horner, I find no attempt has been made towards researches by digging or opening the ground; the country
people called this farm-house the abbey, but strange to
remark, I cannot find the smallest account of any thing
relating to the antiquity, or history of any part of the
village, and all that relates to the church is what Camden observes; and this the more surprises me, as Marsworth church carries with it the appearance of considerable antiquity, the architecture is a mixture of the Saxon
and Gothic, the internal support of the roof of the
church is a very curious specimen of fine workmanship,
and resembles in miniature that of Westminster-hall; it
appears unimpaired by time, and is most probably formed
of the same durable oak.   To this roof I attach considerable import, and the doors of most of the old pews
are of most curious and ancient workmanship.

   In the upper parts of the windows of the church are
the relics of some excellent stained glass, which was
once very plentiful, but dreadful delapidations have been
committed on it.   Parts of the flooring of the church
are paved with Roman bricks, ornamented with figures,
birds and tessellations.   A large tomb, near the altar,
has been dreadfully mutilated, from the remains of what
is left, it must have been a master-piece of art; on the
floor of the tower of the church are the remains of the
capital of a column of beautiful workmanship, composed
partly of the vine and its tendrils, which is now most
ruthlessly knocked about; the appearances on the inside

of the church confirm me in my former conjectures, that in this spot lie many hidden treasures of antiquity. In Marsworth church are some monuments of the families of West and Seare; the last heir male of the Wests died in 1700; on an altar tomb belonging to this family is an engraved plate of brass, on which is represented a man in armour, lying in a bed, death striking him with a dart, his wife and children kneeling by the bedside, and a divine in canonicals at the foot of the bed; the inscriptions are obliterated, and the tomb partly sunk into the earth; no record is legible of whom the person was it was built for, and to judge from its appearance it must be many centuries old. The great tithes of this parish are vested in the Master and Scholars of Trinity College, Cambridgeshire, who are patrons of the vicarage; the family of the late Sir Drummond Smith, Bart. are lessees of the great tithes under the College. The manor of Marsworth de la Haye, after the death of Mrs. Henrietta Seare, became the property of Edward Barker, Esq.

Marsworth is seven miles from Aylesbury, and two from Tring; Sir John Cobham having surrendered the manor of Marsworth to Edward III., that king gave it to his shield-bearer, Thomas Cheney, ancestor of the Cheney's of Drayton Beauchamp; it reverted to the crown, and Richard II. granted it to the family of Brian, who about 1570 sold the whole, part of it to the Wests. There are now three manors, Marsworth de la Haye, Marsworth cum Goldington, the property of the late Sir Drummond Smith, Bart., and another manor belonging to St. Thomas's hospital.

From the elevation I have noticed at the back of this church, we were presented with one of Nature's grandest pictures, the eye wandering over an immense panoramic display of scenery, in all its variety and magnificence.

The towers of Pittlesthom and Ivinghoe churches are
seen to the southward, rising above the woods, that surround those villages; a succession of spires present
themselves in the valley, or on the brows of the adjacent
hills. Eddesborough village and knoll, on which stands
its antique church, is observable, rising amid the valley
in a north-east direction; while woods over each alter-
nate distance, constitute a display of most delightful
scenery, all the way to the town of Leighton Buzzard;
whose church-spire protrudes itself above a considerable
eminence, on which that town is situated; surrounded
by a redundance of noble timber. Beyond this, on a
fine day, the eye can discern the down leading to Brick-
hill Magna and Stoke; the valley to the west is bounded
by the Chiltern Hills, which we have before spoken
of. On the opposite side of the vale, are the hills of
Seabrook, Cheddington, and Mentmore, and the Grove
Woods, which range all the way to Burcot in a northerly direction, and divide this valley from the vale of
Aylesbury. The hills just before noticed, to the east of
Marsworth, form a part of Buckinghamshire, on a part of
which Ashridge park is situated.

Passing away from thence in a south-east direction,
the view embraces the Albury and Penley Hills, which
rise in bold and sweeping masses, crowned on their summits, with a luxuriant variety of forest timber. From these
points an opening presents itself, which leads towards
Northchurch and Berkhamsted; in the opposite direction
they range on to Tring park, whose summits form several grand knolls, apparently overhanging that town, which
lies in a sort of narrow glen, or ravine, beneath it; as the
eye wanders through the lower parts of these hills, it is
gradually conducted to a view of the meres or reservoirs

below the village, where the combination of objects-form
a beautiful picture.

Aylesbury is distinctly seen, though at seven miles distance, to which a branch of the Grand Junction bears its
way through the valley before us. This stream, and the
navigable feeder to Wendover, are alternately seen meandering through the rich garden beneath. Hedge-rows
traversing the different pastures, at length fall into each
other's focus, and form a concatenation of Sylvan scenes
to the extremity of the horizon.

The resevoir of Wilston is also discernable in the
valley; this immense expanse of country is bounded on
the right of Marsworth by the bold knoll at Cheddington, which rising abruptly above Seabrook-bridge,
brings the sight to a review of the scenery before described.

Remaining for some hours on this charming brow,
and sketching every object that presented itself, we found
most abundant materials, the harvest was getting in,
and the loaded teams were passing in a quick succession ;
the labourers in the wheat field, with gleaners following,
were all in motion, where the corn had been cut down ;
on the other side of us, reapers were trimming down
the standing crops in one field, while in another a fresh
groupe were mowing of beans. Village lasses appeared
in the returning carts bringing refreshments to the sturdy
husbandmen, who with backwardly inclined heads
were seen lifting to their parched lips the much-longed-
for grateful jorum.

The morning was as lovely as the scene was enchant-
ing, and the succession of fine weather had put the
farmers in good temper with themselves; the whole village was in motion, and it might properly be styled
Natures' holiday. Air and exercise, the best friends to

View from Mentmore Village.—Bucks.

health, had invited us to partake of our farmer's rural
fare; placing a few sheaves round our banquet, with the
lasses for our carvers, we made a sumptuous meal upon
our friend's bacon, beef, and plumb-pudding.

The intense heat of weather, and its long continuance,
had for some time past made a fall of rain very desirable, and towards four o'clock, we were highly gratified
by seeing a long scroll of clouds passing in a dense form,
from the distant horizon over the vale beneath; as it
approached us, the elements assumed a deep-toned purple, tinged with a variety of hues, the valley gradually
became enveloped in a " *darkness visible*," exhibiting a
grand and imposing effect; as the clouds neared our
station, they became a strong contrast to the light-
coloured stone of Marsworth church, on which, and its
surrounding wood, a gleam of light was gliding over.

The scene was grand beyond expression, the light that
illumined the church and village, broke in a soft tone
upon the land beneath, from whence gliding up the
brow on which we were standing, suddenly threw a
broad and strong lustre on the wheat-field and its
attendants; a second picture here presented itself, and
that serenity which predominated but a short time before,
was suddenly contrasted by another species of composition.

The harvest carts were now trotting off the hill, and the
gleaners in full run across the stubble, all participated in
the rich effect of the light, and gave a most animated and
interesting finish to the scene; as the storm advanced, and
the lightnings flashed, the horses became unruly, and
even poor Tray, with tail between his legs, was seen
creeping through the " pityless pelting of the storm."
A few minutes carried us from this conflict of the elements, to the hospitable habitation of our host the farmer.

E

Marsworth, laying nearly on the boundary line of the two counties of Herts and Bucks, partakes of the properties of each soil ; chalk, strong loam, and gravel ; the dress they prefer for their land, is rubbish from old buildings, and, when they can get them, old woollen rags ; just below the surface of the earth they get the Hurlock stone, which about these parts are used in making foundations, and paving farm-yards and outbuildings ; eighteen inches below this stratum, is found a hard rocky stone, with which they mend their roads ; it is also applicable to burning for lime. The inhabitants of the county are much indebted to the exertions of their last sheriff for his indefatigable attention to the improvement of the roads from Tring and Berkhamstead, across a most wretched country to Amersham, Chesham, &c. His laudable example appears to have convinced the residents and farmers of these parts, how much more their interests and accommodations would be consulted by keeping the highways in a respectable condition than by suffering their carts, as formerly, to labour, axle-deep, in the ruts.

At Marsworth there is a toll-house on the Grand Junction, from whence the canal declines to its level, below the Cow-roast; altogether there are seven locks here, and three on the Winslow-feeder, and the rise of water, from the level, is about eighty feet ; there are also five reservoirs about these parts, viz. three at Marsworth, one at Weston, and another at Wilstone. These extraordinary reservoirs of water allow of a plentiful supply to all branches of the canal, and as Marsworth is so considerably above both levels, it requires all possible economy to preserve it from an useless waste. By the beneficial operations of the steam-engines they are enabled to save all that water which would otherwise be lost.

We shall hereafter have to detail some particulars of

that wonderful machine, to whose powers, as a manufacturing country, we are in no small degree indebted for
our present opulence and commercial superiority.

In the spring of the year there is a general stoppage,
along the whole line of the canal, for the purpose of
cleansing the bottom ; at this time the stream is drained
into its reservoirs and other channels : and in one week
the Herculian task of removing myriads of filth, mud, and
rubbish, from its bottom, is accomplished, through a distance of nearly an hundred miles.

BUCKINGHAMSHIRE.

As we have entered this county by the village of
Marsworth, it may not be amiss to give some little account of its history, agriculture, and rivers.

The whole of Buckinghamshire, at the time of the
Roman invasion, appears to have been in possession of
the *Catticuchlani;* there is reason to believe that its
western parts had, at no very distant period, been peopled
by the *Ancalites,* whose name is apparently derived from
the *Uchelitwys,* or the inhabitants of high grounds ; thus
called from their relative situation to the *Taveini,* the appellation of the tribe residing in the low grounds near the
rivers Thame and Thames. Camden was of opinion,
that the inhabitants of this county were the ancient
Cassii; which is very probable, not only because there
are some plain remains of the name in Casho hundred,
and Cashiobury, in Hertfordshire, but in their King Cassibelin or Cassivelaun, whose name implies the King of
the Cassii. They were a warlike people, and had made

E 2

such proof of their courage in conquering part of the county of *Dobuni*, their neighbours on the west, that when Cæsar landed, the Britons unanimously chose Cassibelin their king, to be their generalissimo against the Romans, whom he so manfully opposed, that they were forced to retire into Gaul with little or no advantage.

Cassibelin being thus rid of a foreign enemy, turned his arms upon his own countrymen, the Trinobantes, who had favoured the Romans' attempt, and in a fight killed Imanuentius their king, which forced Mandubratius his son to fly to Cæsar, who then lay in Gaul, for his protection.

The Romans having now gotten a glorious pretence to restore a confederate, hastened again into Britain, the next spring, bringing Mandubratius with them. Cassibelin vigorously opposed their landing, but being often repulsed, and at last beseiged in his own city, he found himself necessitated to beg a peace, which, by Comius's means, he easily obtained upon these conditions, viz. that Mandubratius, being restored to his kingdom, should be suffered quietly to enjoy it; that he should give hostages to secure his submission for the future; and pay a yearly tribute to the Roman treasury; and so Cæsar departed, leaving the kings of Britain in the full execution of their former sovereignty, in which they continued until Aulus Plautius subjected them to the imperial power under Claudius Cæsar.

Buckinghamshire, under the Saxons, who divided this part of Britain into seven kingdoms, was part of the kingdom of Mercia; it received the name of Buckingham from them, not so much from the beech trees, which grew then so plentifully in these parts, and were called Buccum, as Camden conjectures, as from the abundance of deer which were found in the woods with which this county was covered; Spelman says, *Buc* in their language, signifies *cervus*, a buck or hart.

· Buckinghamshire is bounded on the north by Northamptonshire; on the east by the counties of Bedford, Hertford, and Middlesex; on the south is Berkshire and Surrey, and on the west by Oxfordshire. In the general view of its agriculture, it is reported to be 45 miles in length, 18 in breadth, and 138 in circumference; it contains about 518,400 acres, 8 hundreds, 16 market towns, · 185 parishes, about 21,000 houses, and 107,440 inhabitants.

The southern parts are bounded by the Chiltern hills, which are composed of chalk intermixed with flints, of the course of which through this county we have already given a detail. The vale of Aylesbury spreads through the middle of the county, furnishing a rich pasturage to vast quantities of cattle, its amazing fertility being chiefly employed in the support of dairy and grazing systems. In the vicinity of the Chiltern hills, where the soil is flinty and light, and inimical to production without much labour, the utmost care is bestowed on the business of husbandry; every variety of materials that will either constitute or increase manure, is carefully collected, and applied with judgment; improved modes of culture are readily adopted, and the general management of the land is praise-worthy and judicious. In the more northern division of the county this picture is reversed; the astonishing produce of the meadows rendering exertion less necessary, the farmer has suffered his indolence to overpower his reason, and content with the evening mist and the morning dew, neglects the means of improvement.

The soil of this county is principally composed of rich loam, strong clay, chalk and loam upon gravel; its application in the Chiltern district is to the growth of wheats, barley, oats, beans, and sainfoin. The northern division, as before observed, is chiefly applied to pasture and meadow, with a small portion of arable; the butter made on the dairy farms is mostly sent to the London market, and contracted for by the dealers half-yearly; the average weight produced weekly from each cow, is eight pounds in summer, and six in winter; in some of the dairies, a very useful machine, called a mill-churn, has been introduced; it is worked by a horse, and saves an infinity of manual labour.

In other dairies a barrel-churn is used, with two handles, turned by two men, who make from six to seven score pounds of butter at one churning; the skim and butter milk is made use of to fatten pigs. In the county there are also a number of calves suckled, and at Aylesbury and its vicinity they are famous for rearing early ducks: there are many curious tales related of the methods adopted by the gossips for promoting an early hatch of these fowls, but certain it is, let the Lent assizes fall as early as may be, the Judges, who go this circuit, always have a supply of young ducks placed on their table, and who, with counsel and solicitors regularly going the Norfolk circuit, are entertained at the expence of the high-sheriff of the county, a circumstance which renders the sheriffalty somewhat expensive. This is the only county in England that has the honour of feasting the bar at the expense of the sheriff, excepting the county of Cambridge, where the custom has prevailed from time immemorial: if it be an honour, I am inclined to think that gentlemen who have to hold the office, would willingly dispense with it.

For ploughing and all laborious agricultural operations, horses are preferred to oxen: in the southern parts, the swing and high-wheel ploughs are chiefly used; in the northern division, the loose handle swing, and low wheel ploughs are worked by five or six horses in a line. The progress of agricultural improvement is considerably checked on many estates, by the restrictive conditions in which they are leased, the tenants being confined to two or three crops and a fallow, with a prohibition from the growing of clover and green food ; the manures are marl, peat ashes, yard and rabbits' dung, lime, chalk, woollen rags, and rubbish of old buildings ; the two last of which are in high request in the southern parts.

The generality of farms are from £60 to £250 a year; there are some few as high as £500 and up to £1000. The principal manufactories are those of paper and lace; the latter is the constant employment for the lower classes of females. The farmers in this county have been much benefited of late years by the water conveyance for their hay to the London market, which nearly averages double what it used to fetch before the Grand Junction stream passed through the county.

The principal rivers are the Ouse and the Thame; the Ouse enters Buckinghamshire on the western side, passes Water-Stratford, and flows in a devious course to Buckingham ; thence winding to the north through a rich tract of meadow land, pursues its way to Stony-Stratford, Newport Pagnell, and Olney, soon afterwards turning suddenly to the east, it leaves the county. The Thame rises near Marsworth, and flowing through the vale of Aylesbury from east to west, enters Oxfordshire near the town of Thame. The mouth of the river Thame being choaked up, and the channel narrowed for want of cleansing, two commissioners of sewers were directed, in the early part of last century, to report upon it; but nothing effectual was done, in consequence of disputes between the commissioners and the land owners. The nuisance having at last so much increased, that the neighbouring part of Buckinghamshire frequently exhibited the appearance of a lake for months together, a new commission was sued out in 1797, under which the object, so long desired, has been effected, by removing the obstructions and restoring the ancient channel. The hay harvests are now secured from risk, and the adjacent country rendered salubrious. The river Thame abounds with eels, which are claimed by the King; its other fish are pike, perch, chub, roach, and gudgeons.

Buckinghamshire is in the diocese of Lincoln, with the exception of six parishes, belonging to the see of Canterbury, and four, to the diocese of London. It sends fourteen members to parliament; pays twelve parts of the land tax; provides the militia with 560 men; and is the first county taken in the Norfolk circuit.

Among the eminent characters who have resided in this county, was John Hampden, Esq., the celebrated patriot; he was born in the year 1594. His family are supposed to have been originally Saxon, and the most ancient in this county, where they had great possessions in the reign of Edward III.; at the age of fifteen he was sent to Magdalen college, Oxford, whence he removed to one of the inns of court; and though often the companion of the gay and dissipated, acquired a considerable knowledge of the laws. The vivacity and cheerfulness of his conversation became the means of his attaining an extensive acquaintance; but the peculiar vigour of his understanding remained concealed, till the period when he contested the legality of the rate called *ship-money*. His opposition to this obnoxious measure rendered him popular; the gratitude of a whole people was excited by his conduct; for in his steady defence of individual right, they discovered the safeguard and the surety of their own.

" The eyes of all men," says Clarendon, " were fixed
upon him as their *pater patræ*, and the pilot that must
steer the vessel through the tempests and rocks which
threatened it." He now became the firm supporter of the
measures employed to counteract the designs of the King;
and by his discernment, spirit, and address, he was soon
advanced to the head of his party. On the commencement of the civil war, he was one of the first to appear
in arms, and shortly afterwards engaged the royal troops
at *Brill,* in this county. His bravery was as conspicuous
as his abilities, and in several skirmishes his success was
favourable; but at length, on the 18th of June, 1643, in an
action with prince Rupert, at Chalgrove-field, in Oxfordshire, he received a mortal wound with a bullet, the shot
entered his shoulder and broke the bone : after suffering
extreme pain for six days, he expired to the great sorrow
of every friend to his person and principles. In the de-
lineation of his character by the Earl of Clarendon, his
reach of capacity, penetration, judgment, and solidity of
understanding, are strongly marked. " His industry and
vigilance," observes the Earl, " were neither to be tired out
nor wearied by the most laborious, nor his understanding to be imposed upon, by the most subtle and sharp."

In taking our farewell of the vale of Aylesbury, we
cannot omit noticing Mr. Ellman, a resident grazier of
this part, who has long been celebrated for bearing away
the prizes of the Bedford, Somerville, and Smithfield
cattle shows.

————◆————

From Marsworth we pass to Seabrook, where we
cross the canal, and for a short period of time lose
sight of its course. There is another road to Leighton
Buzzard, by Ivinghoe, Slapton, &c., through the valley,

but as our return will be by those villages, we shall give some account of them in their proper places.

Cheddington, is a long, straggling village, on a considerable hill above Seabrook-bridge; at the left of the road is its parish church, pleasantly situated on an eminence, and commanding views of the surrounding scenery.

From the extremity of this village, the country opens to another branch of the vale of Aylesbury, which is exactly characterized in the manner we have seen before. The road from thence to Mentmore is by no means in so good a condition as that which we had hitherto passed.

On the left, as we ascend the hill of Mentmore, is Berrysted-house, said to have been the seat of Henry de Blois, bishop of Winchester, brother to King Stephen; it is now a farm-house belonging to the Earl of Bridgewater. In the parish church, which is a handsome Gothic building, are some memorials of the family of Duncombe, who had a seat near here called Barley-end-house, the property of their representative Mrs. Lucy. On the north side of the chancel is an ancient altar-tomb, with effigies of the deceased, said to have been that of a brother of King Stephen, meaning, perhaps, the above Henry de Blois. Browne Willis, the antiquarian, supposes it to be the tomb of Peter Chaceport.

Berrysted-house is a place celebrated in the annals of ignorance and credulity for having once been the terror of its inhabitants. Whilst occupied a few years since by a farmer, his different friends visiting him at that time, were continually kept upon the *qui vive;* the dreadful noises which were confined to a particular room, are said frequently to have caused his guests to alarm the family at midnight. Some very ludicrous circumstances occurred here to a newly married couple, who had gone to Berrysted to pass the honey-moon :—" Ever-valued cour-

. tesy !" which not only gave the happy couple the best
bed-room, but at the same time a spice of its horrors.
The bride, a brisk widow of about forty, and of some
ponderosity, happened to be betrothed to a widower, a
slender, honest, jovial fellow, who cared as little about
the "hows and whens of this life," as any man in the
three kingdoms, provided he had a plentiful replenishing
of his brown jug. This blade had, it seems, brought his
wife by the stage-coach to Leighton, from whence he
conducted her across the country to Mentmore by field-
paths; evening coming on, and with it a storm, the lady
was subjected to the terrible effects of occasionally hob-
bling, ancle-deep, through the ploughed grounds, and was,
by the time they reached Berrysted, completely drenched
with rain. Tired and exhausted with fatigue, the fair
one proposed an early supper, with which her host as
kindly accommodated her. After a hearty meal, the
lady retired ;—but alas! not to rest. Rest was completely out of the question ; mine host and his guest, who
had not seen each other for many years, now set in for
the evening, when

> " Swallow after swallow came
> And then they swore 'twas summer."

Hospitality, the old British farmer's boast, was here at its
height; each draught of the nut-brown increased their
hilarity, until the alarm-bell warned them of the " witch-
ing time of night ;" a parting jug was mutually agreed
on, when as they were pledging each other, a most tre-
mendous crash, like that of a rolling-stone, falling from
the top to the bottom of the stairs, was heard, and ere the
terrified topers could have time to jump up, the door flew
open, and presented to their astonished eyes the weighty
bride, *sans cap*, *sans coats*, *sans shoes*, *sans every*

thing, with the simple exception of her *chemise.* Bruised
from head to foot, and the blood copiously flowing, her
eyes standing aghast, and vociferating " *I have seen him!*
I've seen him! I have seen him!" the terrified fair one
fell into the arms of the female servant, who by this time
had reached the parlour. The scene, as might be expected,
terminated in an histeric fit; hartshorn, vinegar, and
the usual remedies, after an hour's application, at length
restored the fair sufferer to her reason, when she was
anxiously requested to explain what had occasioned her
fright: she repeated her former ejaculations, emphatically
declaring, that she had, by the glimmer of the taper's
light, positively seen ———— What? ————
a rat running across the floor! Now as the farm happened to be plentifully stocked with those quadrupeds,
there can be no doubt but that these were the terrible
phantoms that disturbed the slumbers of the visitors of
Berrysted!

Mentmore village is situated on the crown and around
the base of a conical hill, the top of which forms a circular plot of ground, and has much the appearance of a
Roman station ; it belongs to the hundred of Cotslow,
in the deanery of Mursley, and the living is in the gift of
Trinity college, Cambridge.

Mentmore church stands on the left of the road, at the
eastern extremity of the green; the views from hence
are very delightful, and command the surrounding country
in every direction. Wing-park, a pleasant spot, is seen
in a north-west direction, with part of the vale of Aylesbury. On the south-east side of this hill, the whole range
of the Chiltern hills, and in the vale beneath them, the
Grand Junction canal is viewed in all its windings.

The descent from Mentmore is exceedingly steep, and
the road very bad, until we reach Leyburn, a long,

Leighton Beaudesert. — Beds.

Drawn by I. Hassell.

straggling village, situated on two angles of a spacious common, cheerless, swampy, and miserably poor. The road now assumes a fresh soil, and from a rag-stone and clay we entered a deep sandy country ; on the right is Grove church, and a gentleman's seat and grounds, delightfully situated on an eminence. A smart shower hastened our pace, and at three miles from Leyburn we entered Leighton Beaudesert, by a bridge over the Grand Junction, for a late dinner, with as excellent an appetite as air and exercise generally produce.

The other road, as before observed, is through the valley from Marsworth, by Ivinghoe, a little market-town, surrounded with woods, from thence to Aston-green, and by Slapton to Leighton.

Leighton Beaudesert, or as it is sometimes erroneously written, Leighton *Buzzard*, is a market town on a considerable eminence above the Grand Junction canal, which passes within a furlong on the west side of it, where a rivulet separates the counties of Bedford and Bucks. The commodities sold in the market are cattle, corn, bone-lace, and straw plat, and there is a considerable traffic from its neighbourhood for hay, and milch cows, to supply the metropolis ; the hay is conveyed in barges up to eighty tons burden, and the channel of the canal is always kept of sufficient depth for craft of that tonnage.

There are between three and four hundred houses in this town, and nearly 2000 inhabitants. Here is a most respectable quakers' meeting, whose excellent moral maxims cause but very few of that fraternity to become poor. If a member turns idle, drunken, or otherwise depraved, he is immediately expelled the society, and their poor are principally maintained at their own homes. There is also an alms-house here for eight poor women,

who have each an apartment, clothes, fuel, and 2s. 6d.
a week; and donations, to the amount of £22, annually
distributed in bread to the indigent parishioners.

Leighton Beaudesert has two handsome pieces of antiquity; the first we shall notice is its pentangular cross,
supposed to have been erected about 700 years ago, but
by whom, or for what purpose, cannot be discovered.

From the court-roll of the town it appears, that some
time, about 1650, it was presented at the court-leet, as being
in such a ruinous state that it greatly endangered the lives
of persons passing near it. On this occasion it was ordered to be repaired, and a tax of 4d. levied on every inhabitant to defray the charges. The height of the cross
is 27 ft. 2 in. from the top of the stone work to the base-
ment, which is 7 ft. 4 in. from the ground, and consists of
five rows of steps rising from the earth; the centre pillar
which supports the arch, is 8 ft. 2 in. high, and 1 ft. 1½ in.
wide on the side fronting the largest angle; the upper
story is disposed into five niches, and adorned with pinnacles at the corners—one of these is destroyed; within
each niche was a statue. The first a bishop; another
appears like a virgin and child; a third seems to be St.
John the Evangelist; the others are so much mutilated,
that even conjecture cannot be hazarded. The whole
height, from the lowest base to the top of the vane, is
38 ft.; it is built of stone, and is situated in an open area
nearly opposite to the market-house.

The church is a large antique building, and, by the various grotesque carvings, which are scattered about it, is
supposed to have been built at the same period as the
cross, and is constructed with the same sort of stone; at
the intersection rises a square tower, surmounted with a
spire; the whole being 193 ft. in height.

The township consists of five hamlets; the greater part

Three Locks: Stoke Hammond. – Bucks.

Drawn by I. Hassell.

of the land is open field, about 300 acres of common
belong to the parish, on which the poor obtain turf, &c.
About half a mile from hence are the remains of a Roman
camp. From this and other circumstances, Leighton
Beaudesert is supposed to have been the Saxon *Lyzeam-
burgh*, taken with several more towns from the Britons
by Cuthwolf.

The regular cross-road from the two universities of
Oxford and Cambridge passes through Leighton; the
distance between each place is 89 miles. From this town
we take the lower road, by Linslade, to Fenny-Stratford.
At the lowest part of Leighton, the road passes on the
right into the valley, and we course the banks of the
Grand Junction until we reach Linslade, at two miles
distance, on the left of which is the seat of Lady Lovatt.
Linslade rocks have a picturesque effect, and form an
elevated ridge above the beds of both the canal and the
rivulet; at the very top of the hill are placed two ribs of
a large whale. The opposite downs range in very noble
sweeps, and pass away to Great Brickhill. The rivulet,
in its course, is both a receiver and feeder to the Grand
Junction, and accompanies the navigation all its way to
Newport Pagnell, where a branch of the Ouse river
forms a junction with it, coming from Buckingham,
by Stony-Stratford, to Newport.

We have now to pass over a continued sandy soil
until we reach Stoke Hammond; here there is a considerable rise and fall in the navigation, by three locks, the
elevation of water in each lock being from 17 ft. to 21 ft.
The scenery becomes very interesting at this place, which
is in the parish of Soulsby, from whence there is a rivulet
which serves as a feeder to the canal; from the country
about this part there is an immense quantity of hay shipped for the London market. The usual price of the

carriage seems on an average to be 20s. a ton, but owing
to the great drought of last year, and the exorbitant
prices, they made an additional demand of 2s. per ton.
The commercial boats used in navigating the canal are
long and narrow, and admit of two entering a lock at the
same time; an economical principle by which they save
the double dues and toll at the pay-gates; for what
reason I am withal unacquainted, but the country people
in these parts call them *monkey boats :* the passage boats
are much broader, and have every accommodation for
passengers, travelling usually at the rate of thirty miles
a day. There is another description of boats, called *fly
boats,* which are allowed to travel night and day on the
Grand Junction canal ;—these boats bring with them
Manchester goods, and all articles which require particular care, and like the monkey boats, generally go in
pairs, to save lockage, &c. The following are the rates
chargeable on single boats :

Charges to be paid by Boats passing single on this Canal, as a Compensation
for the Loss of Water occasioned thereby.

⁜ *Boats having been guaged or weighed at Paddington or Braunston, may
pass in the Night, upon paying 5s. in addition to the following Rates.*

	£.	s.	d.
From Paddington to the Thames, 6s. each way	0	12	0
From Paddington to any place short of Rick- mansworth lock, 5s. each way	0	10	0
From Paddington to Wendover, or any place between Wendover and Rickmansworth lock, 6s. each way	0	12	0
From Paddington to Aylesbury, 9s. each way	0	18	0
From Paddington to any place between Ayles- bury and Buckingham, 10s. each way ...	1	0	0
From Paddington to Yardley, or Northampton, the Grand Union canal, or any interme- diate place, 11s. each way	1	2	0

From Paddington to Braunston, 12s. each way £1 4 0

From Braunston to Northampton, or any intermediate place, 4s. each way 0 8 0

From Braunston to Fenny-Stratford, or any
place between thence and Aylesbury,
inclusive, 10s. each way 1 0 0

From Braunston to any place between Aylesbury and Uxbridge, 11s. each way 1 2 0

From Braunston, or the Grand Union canal, to
Brentford, 15s. each way 1 10 0

From Northampton to Leighton, or any place
between, 4s. each way 0 8 0

From Fenny-Stratford to Tring, or any intermediate place, 5s. each way 0 10 0

From Fenny-Stratford to Berkhamstead, or any
intermediate place, 7s. each way 0 14 0

After passing these locks at Stoke Hammond, the navigation inclines to the north-east, and is buried between
woods which line the base of some high hills, forming
a perfect Sylvan appearance.

On the evening we passed this place, it wore a deep tone
of colour, from the rich shadows that were thrown over
the scene by the effect of the setting-sun. A road to the left
from hence leads to Buckingham; the opposite way carried
us through the village of Stoke, a very rural spot, pleasantly situated amidst some lofty timber; a short distance
brought us again on the banks of the canal, which we tra-
versed until we reached Water Eaton. The opposite hills
of Magna Brickhill, continue a back ground of considerable beauty, diversified with hanging woods, sandy rocks,
and rich corn fields, and communicate a peculiar interest
to the surrounding scenery. At a mile from Water
Eaton we reached Fenny-Stratford, a town dependent on

F

its thoroughfare towards the north, and its navigation to the south. This town forms the appearance of a cross, its greatest length reaching towards the road to Leighton ; it stands on the old Roman military way, called Watling-street. The celebrated hills opposite this town, of Bow Brickhill, Little Brickhill, and Brickhill Magna, are, according to Camden, all upon the Watling-street. I should rather imagine that learned antiquarian must mean, that Little Brickhill, through which the high road passes, was on the Roman way, and that the other two villages were Roman stations of some description, and commanded the passage at this spot, which, from their elevated situations, they most certainly might.

Fenny-Stratford is a small decayed market town, in the parishes of Bletchley and Sympson. The chapel, which is in the former parish, having been dilapidated ever since the reign of Elizabeth, was re-built by subscription procured by Browne Willis, esq., the celebrated antiquarian, who laid the first stone in 1724, and the chapel was dedicated to St. Martin, which strongly indicates that whimsical disposition for which he was remarkable, because his grandfather died on St. Martin's-day, in St. Martin's-lane. Within the rails of the communion-table lie the remains of this gentleman. Mr. Willis's corpse was attended to the place of interment, at his own request, by the corporation of Buckingham, to which town he bore a singular affection. By his will he bequeathed a benefaction for a sermon to be preached in this chapel, on St. Martin's-day, and he requests that the rector of Bletchley may never have the cure of Fenny-Stratford ; but he directs that if the rector will contribute six pounds a year towards his salary, he shall have the appointment of the curate, and he requests his heirs to augment the curacy. It does not appear that this has ever been done, nor has the

Fenny Stratford — Bucks.

Drawn by I. Hassell.

rector acquired the patronage of the chapel, which still belongs to Mr. Willis's family. To the manusoript collections, as well as the printed work of Mr. Willis, the public are much indebted for his history of the town of Buckingham. His large collections towards a history of the county, are now in the Bodleian library at Oxford. His church notes are chiefly valuable as recording many monumental inscriptions, which have since his time been either removed or obliterated. In taste he was certainly deficient, for he passes over without mention the most valuable specimens of ancient architecture, while he dwells with minuteness on the dimensions of the buildings, the number of bells, their inscriptions, &c.

Near to the church is the market-house, a sorry little erection, on the left of the principal street, of which we have annexed a view. The town is situate on a brow, rising from the navigation and the river; it has an excellent inn for accommodation, opposite the church. In this neighbourhood is Stockgrove, the seat of Edward Harmer, esq.

We saw here a number of asses, laden with the same sort of stone that we noticed at Marsworth, fit for making into lime. The church of Bow Brickhill, capping the crown of the hill, and surrounded with an abundance of wood, is a very pleasing object, seen from hence; that village and the range of hills that accompany the eastern side of the Grand Junction, begin to decline in altitude, gradually diminishing until they reach the open valley to the north, where they dwindle into insignificance. It is not improbable that this town takes its name from being contiguous to a fenny country.

It was near Stony that a lock was obliged to be constructed to recover a level for the Grand Junction canal, that was lost between Woolverton and Stoke Hammond.

Being now got upon the Watling-street, of which Stukeley makes the following remarks;---" That it is the direct
road to *Rome*, for take a ruler, and lay it on a map of
Europe, from Chester through London and Dover, and it
makes a straight line with Rome; so the great founders
had this satisfaction, when they travelled upon it, that
they were ever going upon the line that led to the imperial capitol. Our antiquarians are much at a loss, after
torturing of words and languages, to find out the reason
of the name of this street, which is so notorious, that
many other bye-roads of the *Romans*, in different parts of
the kingdom, have taken the same, and it became almost
the common appellative of such roads. My judgment
of it is this ; it is natural to denominate great roads from
the places they tend to, as the *Icening-street*, from the
Iceni ; the *Akemancester*, in Wiltshire, and other places,
the way to *Exeter*, they call the *Exeter-road*, though a
hundred miles off; so the *London-road* is every where
enquired for, as the most remarkable place. Thus
Watling-street, tending directly to Ireland, no doubt was
called the *Irish*-road, that is the *Gathelian*-road, *Gathelin*-
street ; whence our present word *Wales*, from *Gauls*,
warden from *guardian*, &c. Whether there be any thing
in the story of *Gathelus*, as founder of the Irish, I do not
concern myself at present, but their language is called
Gaothela. So Mr. Camden says, the true genuine Scots
own not that name, but call themselves Gaoithel, gaioth-
lac, as coming from Ireland, and that they glory in this
name ; and there is no dispute but this is the ancient appellative of the Irish, which the learned Mr. Edward
Lloyd has turned into *Gwydhelians*, and this name has
superseded that which the *Romans* gave it, (whatever it
was,) and seems to show there was such a road, in the
ancient times of the Britons, as the track of trade between

Ireland and the continent; yet it must be owned, nought
but Roman hands reduced it to the present form."

From Fenny-Stratford, we leave the Watling-street,
and take the road to Newport Pagnel, which leads in
an immediate northern direction, along-side of the
Grand Junction. At a mile from Fenny we cross the
navigation, and continue on an excellent high turnpike
road until we reach Sympson, a pleasant rural village,
with an excellent church ; behind which the river Lovat
is seen winding its course through the adjoining valley.
The country and its cottages again begin to assume
a very picturesque appearance. Walton church stands in
a fertile valley on our right; from whence ranging
into an open country, the river takes a circuitous passage by Woolston Magna, and then shapes its course to
Newport Pagnel. The navigation, which had accompanied the road all the way from Fenny to Sympson, on
our left, was now hidden for a short time by some eminences, (for hills they can scarcely be called,) at a distance from the road. A mile and a half onward carried
us to the village of Woughton, a truly pictorial spot,
and which brought to my recollection, from its affinity in
appearance, those beautiful scenes in Wales and Cumberland, I have paused on, with delight.

On the top of the hill, at the extremity of the village,
is the church; the composition at this spot, combines in
itself a very pretty picture, indeed the whole road offered
a succession of rural subjects, but the navigation and
scenery not uniting together, much of the interest was lost ;
it still continued on our left, passing under the base of
some well wooded eminences, until we reached Woolston
Magna, another pleasant village, and then goes by Woolston Parva, and at two miles farther reaches Willen.

The church at this place is a brick building, and very singular in its appearance; standing on an eminence, it commands some rich scenery.

Two miles from this village, by a pleasant shaded lane, we arrive at Newport Pagnel, a town situated on the side of a small hill, with the rivers Ouse and Lovat traversing its valley. The church is of some antiquity and consequence, with a large tower at its west end, and is dedicated to the Saints Peter and Paul. In the north aisle, in the year 1618, the body of a man was dug up, with all the hollow parts of the bones filled with lead. The lead that was taken out of the skull is now in the library of St. John's College, Cambridge; it is in two parts, and seems to have filled the whole interior of the cranium. The church-yard slopes immediately down to the river, and occupies a considerable space of ground. Newport Pagnel, as it is commonly called from the ancient lord of it, *Fulke Paganel* or *Paynell*, from whom it descended to the Baron Somers of Dudley, who had the castle here, but of which no traces are discoverable, nor particulars to be found; but that it remained a place of strength till the time of the civil wars. Three hospitals were founded here in early times, the one endowed by John de Somerie in the year 1280, for six poor men and women, still survives, having been founded anew by Anne of Denmark, and from her named Queen Anne's hospital; in the church yard are seven alms-houses, built and endowed by John Rivis, citizen and draper of London, affording a comfortable asylum to four men and three women. The labouring classes are chiefly supported by lace-making. " There is scarcely a door of a cottage to be seen during summer but what is occupied by some industrious pale-faced lass; their sedentary trade forbidding the rose to bloom

Newport Pagnell. — Bucks

in their sickly cheeks." It has been said, that more lace is manufactured in this town and its neighbourhood than in all the rest of England.

In the reign of Henry III, Roger de Somerie was dispossessed of his lands for neglecting to obey a summons to receive the honor of knighthood; they reverted in the reign of Edward II. to the Someries; that monarch having conveyed them to Thomas de Botetourt on his marriage with Joan, the sister of John de Somerie, the last male heir. Newport is a good market town, and thoroughfare to Northampton and Leicestershire; its market-day is on Saturdays, and has three fairs in a year, (April 11, June 11, and November 6.) In Stukeley's time, it was neither a borough nor a corporation, though larger than many towns; it gave the title of baron at that period to the Earls of Anglesea. There has been founded here very recently a royal Lancasterian school, for children of all religions. At the extremity of the town, leading to Stony-Stratford, a branch cut out of the Grand Junction, supplies it with water and carriage for its heavy goods; on its banks there are a number of wharfs and spacious warehouses. There are several excellent inns in Newport, but a preference is certainly to be given to the Swan, (Mrs. Higgins's, a widow lady, who keeps it) which is deserving of every encouragement.

The rivers Ouse and Lovat, unite their streams immediately below the town, where the name of the Lovat, which accompanies the navigation all the way from Slapton, is lost, and that river becomes a part of the Ouse.

The road from London to Manchester, Liverpool, and other parts of the north, which passes through Newport, crosses each of those rivers by two bridges.

These bridges from their age, the bad materials of which

they were built, and the action of the immense floods which swell the rivers in winter, had become so ruinous, that in the year 1809 an act was obtained and trustees appointed for taking down the two ancient bridges, erecting new ones in their stead, and widening and otherwise altering their approaches, so as to render them more safe and commodious to the public. For carrying this work into execution the trustees were empowered to raise by mortgages, or by annuities, or both, a sum not exceeding £12,000, to be repaid, together with the interest thereon, by a toll, imposed on all coaches, carriages, horses, and other cattle, passing over the said bridges.

That over the Ouse, called North bridge, may rather be considered a series of bridges, connected with each other by high mounds of earth, inclosed between strong stone walls, built after the manner of Vauban, over which the road is carried.

The whole breadth of water-way of this bridge is 200 feet, and the largest arch is 40 feet; the stone of which it is built is a hard lime-stone, found in the parish of Newport Pagnel, about a mile from the town.

The foundations are built on a solid rock, twelve feet below the surface of the river.

The new bridge over the Lovat, usually called Tickford-bridge, consists of one single arch of cast iron, 60 feet in the span; the abutments are of the same kind of stone as the North-bridge, and are sunk down to the solid rock, at the depth of 18 feet below. In digging the foundations of these bridges a quantity of oak timber was found buried at a considerable depth, which evidently appeared to have been the remains of wooden bridges that had stood on the same spots previous to the erection of the old stone bridges that were lately pulled down.

View at Linford Magna, near Standon Bury, Bucks.

Drawn by I. Hsgold.

London. Pub.d 1. Aug.t 1794 by I. Hsgold, 87. Richard Street. Islington.

Both these bridges were built by Mr. Provis of Paddington, an engineer of celebrity, from his own designs,
they are specimens of durability and pure taste, and highly
ornamental to the entrances of the town either way.

Mr. Praed, the chairman of the Grand Junction committee, has a seat near Newport, called Tillingham.

Generally making our first stage early in the morning,
we rose with the day-break, and from our chamber-win-
dow were presented with a grand effect of the rising
luminary.

The morning dew had enveloped all the lower parts of
the town, down to the river's side, while the upper
stories and the surrounding woods, were brilliantly lighted
up by the rising sun, bursting over the dense vapours,
which but a few minutes before had obscured it. In the
descriptive imagery of our immortal bard—

" The morn in russet mantle clad,
On tip-toe walked o'er yon high eastern hill."

The splendour and sublimity of the breaking of day, with
all the various hues, from grey haziness to streaks of brilliant purple and red, dappled with tawny yellows, are
effects that should be instantaneously copied, and ought
to become the particular care of the artist; for whatever
is coloured on the spot and from nature invariably forms
the best picture.

By the time we had reached Great Linford church,
the sun had made considerable progress in its course, and
exhibited the valley on our right in a luxuriant mantle ;
the distant hills were richly wooded, and receded from
the sight in varied forms. At the furthest extremity of
the valley, and on the brow of a woody knoll, is the
mansion of Colonel Smith, most pleasantly situated, overlooking the surrounding country in every direction. At
two miles distance from Newport, we again fall in with

the navigation, where we derived some idea of the trade carried on upon the Grand Junction; a succession of barges followed each other, freighted with the various branches of traffic, transported from inland manufactories to London.

Fly-boats, heavy barges, and coal-craft, were passing in rapid succession, and seemed to indicate that they had all left their over-night's station nearly at the same time.

The canal here passes to the right of the road, and courses the brow of a small hill for some distance, when we descended to another bridge over the stream, which again crosses the road, and continues in view for some extent along the base of the opposite hill. Hanslop church, at a considerable distance on the highest part of the distant hills, stands conspicuous, its tall tower overlooking the neighbouring country for an immense extent. About fifteen years since, a storm of thunder and lightning destroyed this beautiful tower, which the parish felt very little disposed to re-build, until the county gentlemen interfering, and caused its re-erection according to its former plan. We have often heard of sportsmen hunting the steeple; from the elevated situation of Hanslop church tower, and the openness of the adjacent country, this building seems particularly calculated as a noble land-mark for such an atchievement.

Hanslop is built on the summit of a hill, whence there is a gradual descent on all sides; a situation which corresponds with the reputed etymology of its name from the Saxon word *haën*, and *slope*, a declivity. The village is only remarkable for its church, which was one of the most ancient edifices in the county; it sustains a neat hexagonal steeple, the top of which is nearly 190 feet from the ground; the body of the church consists of a nave and side ailes.

Passing Stone-bridge-house, by a very pleasant road,

The Aqueduct at Wolverton.— Bucks.

Drawn by I. Hassell

shaded with an abundance of lofty trees, we come to the village of Woolverton. The country here burst upon us with peculiar beauty; the scenery on our right presented the navigation passing in long line away to Cosgrove, which terminates in a succession of woods, towering above each other, with the seat of Major Mansell to the left, and Cosgrove church a little more to the right. The Grand Junction is here carried across the valley by an embankment originally built upon arches, but bursting its course, a wooden trough was afterwards substituted, through which the barges were conveyed to either part of the canal. This trough has given way to one made of cast iron, for the special purpose of uniting the channel, the durability of this metal being much greater than that of wood. The artificial channel is much narrower than the usual passage of the navigation, and viewed from the bridge at this village, has a singular appearance. The component parts of the scenery about Woolverton are truly picturesque, and afford a variety of subjects for the pencil. The Ouse river that runs from Old Stratford passes up the vale before us, and under the channel of the Grand Junction canal, where it unites with the river Tone, which comes from Stoke Bruern park, the seat of Mr. Vernon, and then takes its course by Haversham and Standon to Newport Pagnel, in a north-east direction.

While sketching the scene before us, a hare which had just been shot at, passed close by the bridge pursued by a pointer; having been headed by another dog, it returned down the hedge, and making two doubles, went into some rushes on the bank of the navigation, from whence it swam across the canal and made for the woods. By this time the sportsmen had got up with their dogs, who instantly pointed at the rushes; at length they encouraged their pointers to go in among them, when all appeared disappointment; and they observing me at a short distance, probably imagined poor puss had died of her wounds at that spot, and that I had witnessed some person take her away. In full confidence of their opinion, the gentlemen politely addressed me on the subject, when I satisfied them by pointing out the poor creature, who had again been disturbed, and was coursing the opposite valley in a fresh direction, but at too great a distance for their pursuit.

According to Camden, this village was anciently called Wolverington, from the seat of an ancient family so named, whose lands are called in the records, the barony of Wolverington; from them it descended to the Longuevilles, many ages ago; for John de Longueville, who was sheriff of the county (18 Richard II.) had his residence here. It was lately in the possession of Sir Edward Longueville; it was afterwards purchased by the late famous Dr. Ratcliffe, who was so shamefully treated at the death of Queen Anne as to cause his dissolution.

Prior to the present improvement the Grand Junction was passed between Cosgrove and Woolverton by nine locks, which considerably retarded the navigation, and caused the company to contract with some persons at Stony-Stratford for erecting a new embankment across the valley, which was to be made as durable as Warwick-bridge, with similar abutments, the Grand Junction company, reserving to themselves the right of inspecting surveyors and engineers to determine its durability and workmanship; a previous trial of twelve months was also to be allowed the Grand Junction company to prove its solidity. After its erection Mr. Bevan, the engineer, of Leighton Buzzard, being called upon, gave it as his opinion, it would not stand twelve months; his prediction was verified, for in less than six months after its construction, the materials were so indifferent, that a continued leakage of the aqueduct was observable; which occasioned a wag of Stony-Stratford, to observe, " the drainage and droppings of the water were the tears of the contractors of the valley ;"— a joke, the parties, it is said, have never forgiven.

Mr. Bevan suggested, after the blowing up of the embankment, the temporary erection of a wooden trough, until another of iron could be cast, which was undertaken and finished at Heseltine's foundry in Shropshire, and laid down in the place of the wooden one, all in the course of twelve months from the time of the accident.

Mr. Cherry, of Greenbridge lock, near Woolverton, was the first person to observe the disaster, and at eleven o'clock at night had but just time to pull up the stop gates, and let off some of the waste water, before the embankment blew up. He sent off a messenger to apprise the inhabitants of Stony-Stratford of the accident. The consternation soon became general, every inhabitant expecting momentarily his house to be insulated from the effects of the approaching element. The alarm, added to the time of night, caused a dreadful and awful suspense, which only subsided with the day-breaking, when it was observed the valley only was inundated; which cleared off its waters in about three days. Fortunately the graziers lost no cattle of any consequence from its effects.

The devastation occasioned at this spot, by the bursting of the canal, reminds me of a calamity that befel the late Duke of Bridgewater. While prosecuting his favourite undertakings in Lancashire, he had the mortification to witness a breach made by the blowing up of a dam, which instantaneously covered the surrounding country, and it was supposed by all who witnessed

the irruption, that it was completely fatal to the whole
work. Astounded at the event, he sat motionless on the
bank, and petrified with surprise, while viewing the
work of years, ruined in an instant. This was a stroke
of fate that few even of your boasted philosophers could
have withstood—an immense fortune embarked in a speculation, which in an instant appeared blasted beyond
all hopes of recovery. His great mind was now strained
to its utmost bearing, and he determined at the moment
to complete his task or sacrifice all he possessed. He
accordingly mortgaged and borrowed money by every
possible means, placed hundreds of additional hands
to clear away the sand and rubbish which had been
heaped together, and in a short period he had the consola-
tion of beholding, finished, what his perseverance and re-
solution had determined him to follow up. It is still to be
hoped a nations' gratitude will cause to be erected an ada-
mantine statue to perpetuate the memory of this great and
distinguished nobleman, of whom, it may truly be said,
his whole life and fortune were devoted to his country's
welfare.

Woolverton church is a very handsome structure, partly
of a modern Saxon order of architecture, with curious
circular frame-work to hold the glasses. The whole village
and its accompanying scenery are beautiful to a degree.
A mile from hence we enter Stony-Stratford, which
stands upon the old Roman causeway, the Watling street.
It is a populous and well frequented market-town, but
is most vilely paved with stones of various dimensions.
This being the great thoroughfare to Chester, Wales, and
Ireland, it is not a little surprising that it should be
suffered to remain in such a wretched state, and more
so, that the town should not be indicted for neglect of
the highway. Camden and Stukeley differ materially

Stoney Stratford — Bucks.

Drawn by I. Hassell.

London, Pub.d I.st June 1819 by I. Hassell, 41. Richard Street, Islington.

about this town, the former averring it to be the *Lactoro-dum* of the Romans, and the place where Edward I. erected a cross to the memory of his queen, Eleanor of Spain, adorned with the arms of England, Castile, and Leon; as Hollinshed says, he did in all other towns between this and Westminster, where the corpse rested. While on the other hand, Stukeley affirms, Lactorodum to be Old Stratford, on the opposite side of the Ouse to Stony Stratford, and that Queen Eleanor's cross stood a little north of the *Horse Shoe Inn*, pulled down in the Rebellion, which, he says, shews the town was on that side of the bridge in the time of Edward I. In and about this neighbourhood, he also observes, there has been found a number of Roman *coyns*.

Opposite the Cock, the most celebrated inn at Stratford, stands St. Giles's, the largest of the two parish churches; the west end of this building is terminated by a triangular projecting Gothic window of beautiful workmanship; the inside is a miniature of Westminster Abbey; the pillars that support the roof are remarkably small in their circumference, though very lofty. It is a very tasteful building, and does infinite credit to Mr. Irons, the architect of Warwick. It was built in the years 1776 and 1777; it was formerly a chantry, valued at £20 2s. 6d. per annum. On the 19th of May, 1742, the town suffered greatly by fire, nearly two-thirds of the east side were consumed, together with the body of the church of St. Mary Magdalen, but the tower is yet standing. The necessary regulations to preserve the peace are made by two of the neighbouring magistrates, who hold their meetings on the first Friday in every month. From this town a branch of the Grand Junction passes away to Buckingham.

We leave Stony-Stratford by a bridge over the Ouse,

and at the extremity of Old Stratford, take the right
hand road, and again fall in with the canal at Cosgrove,
from whence a road leads to the villa of Major Mansell,
the Priory, and Castle Thorpe.

The navigation courses the valley on our right, taking
a considerable circuit beneath the opposite hills. Here we
come in view of the scenery we had passed through in the
early part of the morning, and have a prominent view of
ʿHanslop tower, and the valley towards Newport; the
brows of the hills are richly cultivated and capped
with noble timber, and every yard of our road became
more interesting and picturesque. Passing through the
village of Yardley-Godwin, we descend into the vale,
where we have a view of the river Tone, and the
navigation, in a serpentine direction, until the scene
is closed up ʹby the opposite woods. At the bridge
over the navigation, a quantity of tall trees form admirable groups, and complete an excellent composition;
rising a considerable hill we enter Grafton Regis, which
gives the title of duke to the family of the ʿFitzroys.
Prior to the Rebellion there was a large mansion here, the
seat of the ancient family of the Widvilles, of which Sir
Richard de Widville, in the time of Edward IV. was
created Earl Rivers and constable of England for life,
which honors he received in consequence of his daughter
Jaquet being married to that monarch. This mansion is
now reduced to a small building, the principal part of
the old house having been taken down.

Anthony Lord Scales, eldest son of the earl, who succeeded his father in the estate, was probably born here.
On the flight of king Edward, he accompanied him into
Holland, with whom subsequently returning he was constituted captain-general of all his majesty's forces, both
by sea and land; he afterwards became an object of

jealousy to Richard Duke of Gloucester, to whom had been committed the guardianship of Prince Edward during his minority. Lord Scales was drawn into a snare at Northampton, his person seized, conveyed to Pomfret-castle, in Yorkshire, and there beheaded. He appears to have been a friend to literature, by his translations of French and Spanish works.

It was in this village that we first saw any alteration in the cottage stile of building; the habitations of the peasants were particularly picturesque, and resemble in appearance those I have seen in the west of England and Wales; they are composed of stone and clay, and thatched. Northamptonshire is famed also for buildings made of a composition of mud, sand, and stubble haum to bind it; after which the surfaces are rough cast, and then whitewashed. It was our fate to pass Grafton Regis on the day appointed by the justices for licencing of victuallers, where we heard the confirmation of one of the most arbitrary acts that ever disgraced an individual armed with power; the recital of which would be too disgusting to our readers. This branch of our laws, I am apprehensive, as it now stands, arms the magistracy with too much discretionary power, for, in the present instance, the pique, and not bad conduct, brought an industrious individual and his large family from a state of comfort to indigence.

At the termination of this village, we are brought in view of Stoke Brian, or Bruerne-park, the seat of Levison Vernon, esq. a most delightful situation, abounding with extensive woods and excellent pasturage. The little river Tone takes its rise in the park, passing in front of the mansion; it forms a sheet of water highly ornamental, intersected with plantations. The house and grounds are seen to the greatest advantage from the brow of the hill of Grafton Regis.

G

The house, which is one of the best in the county, was built by Francis Crane, esq., to whom the estate on which it stands was given, in consideration of money due to him, from the crown, in the time of Charles I.; it is from an Italian design, much in the style of Palladio, began in 1630 and finished in 1636; during which interval he gave an entertainment to the king and queen. It consists of two wings connected with the principal part of the structure by corridores; the columns which support these were formed of a red stone, a colour different from the other parts of the house; but this defect has been remedied by the whole front being cased with white stone.

This Francis Crane, who was the last lay-chancellor of the order of the garter, appears to have had an enterprising mind; for under the patronage of James I. and encouraged by the Prince of Wales, and Villiers Duke of Buckingham, he established a manufactory of tapestry, on an extensive scale, at Mortlake in Surrey, but the extent of patronage was by no means adequate to the undertaking, for by a letter written to the king by Sir Francis, he complains of the royal negligence, of the non-payment of large sums he had expended for the marquis, of £300 besides carriage paid for certain drawings as designs for tapestry, made for Pope Leo X; the subject, the Twelve Months of the Year by Raphael D'Urbino. And he further states his disbursements in the concern had exceeded £16,000, of which, in return, he had received no more than £2,500, and both his estates and credit were so far exhausted, that without further support he should be unable to continue the business one month longer. The royal bounty expected, however was not given, and the trade consequently fell into decay. He died according to the record on his monument in the

Locks ascending, Stoke Bruern, Northamptonshire.

Drawn by I. Pigott.

London Publ.d 1.st July 1842, by I. Pigott. 25, Richard Street. Islington.

church of Stoke Bruerne, in the 82d year of his age,
A. D. 1703.

Descending the hill we come suddenly upon the
seven locks which lifts the navigation from the valley
to the entrance of the tunnel at Stoke Bruerne. The
scenery at the first bridge we pass over is very interesting ; the view of that village, and its church on a wooded
eminence, with the approach to it by the navigation, is
singularly beautiful, and has induced us to introduce
it in the work. It was harvest time, and the avocations of
the farmer appeared on every side. The effect on the landscape was good, and the incidents natural. These combi-
nations charm the spectator in a common scene, but
where a number of local beauties are joined, they give
a consequence to the landscape, and make up a good
subject for the painter; the effects of light and shadow
are the peculiar care of the artist, and often render a
very humble composition of the highest interest. It is
like the graceful carriage of a female, who to a lovely
person and disposition, adds the blandishments of the
Graces.

Every object that encountered our sight, as we passed
to the village, appeared of the picturesque ; the team re-
tiring from the glebe, had its rustic mate and tired
plough boy, with all their paraphanalia, seated on the
leading horses; the navigation attendants and their cattle
were bustling to pass the lock; the freighted boats presented a motly group of passengers on their decks; while
a number of female attendants on the canal horses, reminded me of those hardy Cambrian lasses I have so
often seen following their laborious avocations.

Stoke Bruerne village has a great affinity in appearance to the Welch villages, the buildings very much
resemble them in their make, and brought to my recol-

lection the happy hours I have passed in traversing
those mountainous regions. The church, which is an old
Gothic building, is situated on the highest part of the hill
on which the village stands; and there is an extensive
prospect from the extremity of the church-yard, overlooking the country and the valley we had just passed.
The same view presents itself from the bridge which
we have annexed. At the entrance of the celebrated tunnel, a succession of moving objects occur,
and as it is a resting-place for the navigation cattle, we
anticipated finding some accommodation; our wants
being moderate, we felt highly gratified by our good
hostess announcing her ability to supply us with an
excellent piece of corned beef. The servant being from
home, I undertook the nursery department, and to the
tune of the *Sailor's Lullaby*, rocked a sweet little babe to
its peaceful slumbers, while she provided vegetables to
our repast. The chubby infant reminded me of the
substantial comforts of *Dulce Domum*.

The canal is carried by a level above the tops of those
houses, which are situated at the lower parts of the village,
and appears like a trench cut through a hill, made rather
wider at this place than usual. A quarter of mile brought
us to the entrance of the tunnel, which is faced with brick
and stone, and assimilates in its appearance with the bridges
that are thrown over the stream at the requisite places.
The ground above the entrance is very rugged and picturesque from its inequalities, and being topped with wood.
Several barges were now preparing to enter the excavation; the men throwing off their upper garments and light-
ing up their lanthorn, gave the helm for steerage to the
women, one or two females generally attending each boat;
when ready they loose the tow-rope of the horses, and apply
themselves to the poles, with which they sturdily shove

View from Stoke Bruern Bridge.

the boats through the dark channel. On the top of the hill, just above the navigation, there is a small shed erected for the attendants and cattle that have come over from Blisworth, and are to await the arrival of their proprietor's barges passing through the tunnel from that village. The distance is about two miles and a half under ground, and is usually performed by two men with a loaded boat in two hours and a quarter, but some time less if light or unladen.

We now rise from the tow-path by a considerable ascent, and come in sight of a celebrated sporting country. On our right the view is closed up by a succession of woods and corn fields; on the opposite side of us, we look over the Plane woods, which line the western base of the Tunnel Hill; beyond these are Nun woods; and onward are the Blisworth coverts; more in a south-west direction the country opens to a view of Towcester and Whittlebury forest. The whole of the way to Blisworth, where the apertures had been made for boring the tunnel, the excavated earth has been thrown together in large mounds, and resembles the tumuli of the ancients—it appeared a very rich fat clay, fit for various purposes. At Potterspery, in this country, a course kind of earthenware is manufactured, from a yellow clay, very dense, compact, and of great tenacity. The pots made from it are very brittle, and liable to crack, particularly in frosty weather. As we approach Blisworth the hill continues rising until we come in view of that village; from its highest elevation a noble chain of scenery is presented to the view—the navigation emerging from its obscurity traverses the valley to the left, winding round the base of the hill on which Blisworth stands : it then passes the opposite brow of Gayton, and enters a spacious valley on the right, where, dividing its stream, the lateral branch takes a direction to Northampton, a distance of five miles from Blisworth. Declining a long hill we come in view of the entrance of the tunnel on our left in a considerable dell. Here we have a proof of the ingenuity of man. The level of the canal at this place being so considerably above that in the opposite valley at Stoke Bruerne, it was necessary, as before observed, to give a considerable rise up this hill by means of lockage, to where it was to emerge from the hill at Stoke Bruerne, and from the immense altitude between the levels of the canal at either side of the tunnel, it was deemed impracticable to carry the canal over, probably from the want of water to make a reservoir in so high a country.

However this might be, the committee deemed expedient to cut through the hill, as ultimately it would prove more advantageous and easier of navigation, besides an immense saving of time in passing so many locks as must necessarily have been constructed to carry the boats over it. The undertaking would almost have been deemed miraculous, had there not before been numerous instances of similar excavations. This one was nevertheless attended with considerable disadvantages from the quality of the substratum, and the springs breaking in upon the works, and bringing down quantities of loose earth which choaked the channel, and frequently suspended the progress of the workmen. These difficulties were surmounted in 1806, and the passage formed through the hill was trifling when compared with those which the celebrated Mr. Brindley had to encounter, of which Ignorance and Prejudice were probably not the least.

Mr. Barnes, of Banbury, was engaged by the late Marquis of Buckingham, and the then committee, to conduct the whole line of the canal, as surveyor to the works of the

The entrance into the great Tunnel, from Blisworth, Northamptonshire.

Grand Junction. He also superintended and completed the Blisworth tunnel. He was a strong-minded man, but very illiterate. When the tunnel was finished, the proprietors had a dinner to celebrate the occasion, to which *Old* Barnes, as he was usually called, was invited. On his health being drank, it is said, he returned the compliment in the following words:—" Mr. Chairman and Gentlemen —I beg to return you my thanks—and since we are met together, and the tunnel ended—the least said is the soonest mended." Like the celebrated Mr. Brindley, he made all his calculations by the strength of his memory, and was equally at a loss to explain what he had conceived to any other person ; and from being lowly educated he had no means of conveying to paper his designs, yet would cast up the most intricate accounts in his head without difficulty or error. Before Barnes began the Blisworth tunnel, the goods that came by water to that village were conveyed over the hills to Stoke Bruerne by means of an iron-railway.

The first idea of forming the Grand Junction canal originated with the late Mr. Charles Simpson, of Litchfield. His design was to carry it by quite a contrary route into the Thames, but the interest of the Marquis of Buckingham, and some other large proprietors, caused the canal to be conducted through a part of their estates—to which indeed it has been a profitable conveyance. This navigable cut was began in the year 1792, and completed on the 25th of March, 1805 ; and the company incorporated by an act passed in the 33d year of the reign of his present Majesty.

The tonnage varies from one penny and three farthing to one farthing a mile per ton, occasionally being altered as the committee determine, which is usually to the advantage of those who carry upon it. The wharfs in possession of the company are public wharfs, which any person may land their goods upon by paying the regular charges. Fly-boats, or boats having a permit, are allowed to travel by night; forty-eight hours is the given time for such boats to make their passage from Braunston to London, subject to regulations and fines, if they cannot account for their loss of time on arrival at Paddington.

The general committee consists of thirty-one gentlemen, nine forming a select committee, who regulate all the affairs of the company for the Paddington and Grand Junction canals, both of which are one and the same property. There are also three surveyors along the line of the canal, who have all the businses under their care, with occasional reference to an engineer.

The canal has brought a respectable trade to Blisworth, where are erected an extensive wharfage and warehouses for goods. There are several good inns in the village, which stands on the cross road from Northampton to Towcester. The best general view of the entrance to the tunnel is from the southern extremity of the village, and which we have annexed. From Blisworth we descend a sharp hill, and then recross the canal. The valley on our right towards Northampton opens in a wide expanse, with rising inequalities in various places. A landscape, simply representing smooth surfaces, cannot possess composition. What, for example, can be so uninteresting as a scene with smooth hills, a smooth valley, and a smooth fore-ground; the very want of objects to create animation, reminds me of that deficiency in nature, where we see a systematic regularity of feature with a placidity of countenance, and a vacant imagination.

Pictorial composition consists in uniting a pleasing variety into a whole, where rough objects intersperse themselves on plane surfaces, and communicate to nature all the redundance that can gratify the eye.

It is the contrasted variety in the valley we are now wandering over, that makes it grateful to our vision, and as I have often observed before, the scene is heightened by an excellent effect of light and shade. In the view before us, one uniform light would destroy the landscape, and one uniform shade would precisely have the same effect. Obscurity or glare are equally ruinous to the effect of composition in nature, or on the canvas—foregrounds particularly suffer from a smooth surface, and the same may be said of the first *offskip*. Leaving this delightful *morceau*, we ascend the steep brow of Gayton, and pass its church, from whence we decline its opposite steep brow, and enter by the left the high cross road from Northampton to Foster's Booth, and then take the first turning on the right to Bugbrook.

A rattling shower of rain accompanied us all the way to Bugbrook, a rural spot, with respectable accommodation, and abundant subject for the artist. This town takes its name from a small stream that passes near the church, which is a very pretty building, being a mixture of Saxon and Gothic architecture, with a handsome octagonal spire. From Bugbrook we proceed by an excellent road to Heyford, and have the canal continually in view. Had the evening been fine, we should have enjoyed a delightful ride, as the scenery at every step became more picturesque—the village of Lower Heyford presented an abundance of lofty timber and rural cottages.

On the opposite side of the navigation, and on the brow of a considerable hill, encircled by wood on three sides, is Nether Heyford church, a place once of some consequence. In this church, on a tomb under an in-arched monument, are the portraitures in brass of a man in armour, and a woman in the habit of the times, having their hands joined together, with a Latin inscription, re- cording the memory of Sir Walter Mauntell, and Eli- zabeth his wife, A. D. 1487. At the upper end of the church is an elegant monument, having for supporters two fine statues of Faith and Hope. In the centre are the effigies of a man and his wife, with their offspring ; on a marble tablet, a Latin inscription purports that it was erected to the memory of Francis Morgan, one of the Judges of the King's Bench, who died August the 10th, in the year 1558. In 1553, this Francis Morgan, sat as Judge, and pronounced sentence of death upon the amiable and unfortunate Lady Jane Grey. The cruelty and injustice of which is said to have so affected his con- science, previous to his death, as to bring on insanity, and that in the paroxysms of disease he would cry out, " take away the Lady Jane from me."—This is Holin- shed's account, vol. ii. p. 983.

In this parish was born John Stanbridge, an eminent grammarian. He published the treatises of his day on the science of grammar. Dr. John Preston, commonly called the *Patriarch* of the Puritans, was also a native of this place.

In Horestone Meadow, within the parish of Nether Heyford, and about half a mile east of Watling-street, there was discovered a *tesselated pavement*, covered with mould and rubbish. The tessellæ were of varie- gated colours, and when first opened were as firm and compact as a stone floor; but upon being exposed to the weather the cement became less tenacious, and the tessellæ were easily separated.

From what was found it appeared to have been 15 feet in extent, from east to west; but its diameter, from north to south, is uncertain. Morton presumes it must have been a square, and that it was the floor of a room in some building, of a circular figure, about 20 yards in diameter.

Several lesser rooms or passages at the same time were discovered; the sides of the floors were painted with three straight lines of red, yellow, and green colour. Foundations of walls, and other vestiges of dilapidated buildings, were also visible. In the apartments were found fragments of various antique earthern vessels, which Morton supposes to be a patera and urns, and concludes this was the manor-house of some eminent Roman, and that here some of the family had been interred. To this conjecture Hearne objects, because, as he justly observes, " it was not customary with the Romans to bury in private houses, after the promulgation of the legal code, called the *Twelve Tables*, though the usage was prevalent anterior to that period; and the very allusion of Morton to the testimonies of Isidore and Servius, prove directly the reverse of his position." From what can be collected of this pavement, it was among the inferior kind of tessellated works, distinguished under the appellation *Ropographia*, though Morton, in his sanguine manner, says that it exceeds all the pavements he had seen or read of in England.

This, if not the scite of a Roman *villa*, was evidently that of some *hall* or *mansion*, built for the residence of an officer commanding a district; or it might have been the villa of the general who presided over the adjacent military station, called Benovana.

We had now to take leave of a lovely country, which we highly recommend to the pictorial wanderer, and from the appearance of the distant hills anticipated a continuance of pleasant scenery, in which we were not afterwards disappointed. From the circuitous route a navigation must take in an hilly region, the traveller will imperceptibly be led into the reclusest parts of a country which usually has a romantic appearance. Once more we come on the Watling-street at Stowe Hill, generally called, Stowe-Nine-Churches, where we have a delightful view of the canal looking towards Heyford, and which will be annexed herewith. The opposite view of Weedon church, is also very interesting. The navigation meandering through the valley, loses itself behind the village of Weedon Bec.

Stowe-Nine-Churches takes that appellation from the lord of the manor having had the right of presentation to that number. From the high repute of the monuments in the church of Stowe, we were induced to visit it, though a short distance out of the road. Mr. Pennant has given an account of a monument in this church sacred to the memory of Elizabeth, fourth daughter of John Lord Latimer. He describes it as " the most elegant tomb that this or any other kingdom can boast of." Mr. Pennant has certainly done justice to the merits of the artist, Nicholas Stone; but at the expence of the superior excellencies of Roubiliac, Rysback, and some of our modern sculptors, Mr. Chantry not excepted.

The figure is certainly a fine piece of sculpture, in white alabaster, recumbent on a black slab. The attitude, which is very happily chosen, is the most easy possible, that of a person in sleep; her head reclining on a cushion, is covered with a hood, with a quilted ruff round her neck; one hand is placed on her breast, and the other lies by her side.

The gown which covers her feet flows in the most natural folds, and she lies on a long mantle lined with ermine, fastened at the neck with jewels : all is graceful,

View from Stow-hill, near Upper Heyford, Northamptonshire.

and easy, had it not have been for the preposterous fashion of the times, which was destructive of every beauty, grace, and symmetry.

At the feet is a griffin couchant, holding a shield with the family arms.

This monument was executed by Nicholas Stone, who was a master mason, statuary, and stone-cutter to King James and Charles the Second. From a note of his, preserved by Vertue, it appears that " March 16, 1617, I undertook to make a tombe for my lady-mother of Lord Danvers, which was all white marbell and *touch* (which was a name applied to black stone) and I set it up at Stowe-of-the-Nine-Churches, in Northamptonshire, some two years after—one altar-tombe; for which I had 220 li." To the honor of the present rector of Stowe-Nine-Churches, Stone's monument is guarded and preserved with appropriate care.

Having seen Mr. Chantry's beautiful monument of two children sleeping, exhibited in 1817, at the Royal Academy, I must be allowed to say, it far exceeds this excellent monument by Stone. Mr. Chantry's is not deficient in any branch of the art, possessing all the qualifications of design—simplicity, execution, and a delicate sweetness of expression and innocence.

On the north side of the chancel is a large mural monument, or cenotaph, raised to the memory of Dr. Thomas Turner. This benevolent man expended a large fortune in acts of humanity. The monument records his charities—a statue of whom is represented in his robes as Master of Arts, on a terrestial globe, with a book in his hand; a canopy over his head is supported by two fluted columns of the Corinthian order, and adorned with two large statues, emblematic of Religion and Benevolence. The whole was executed by Thomas Stayner.

We now follow the course of the Watling-street for a mile and a half, when we reach Weedon Bec, which is sometimes called Weedon-on-the-Street. It is a pleasant village, and stands on the confluence of two roads—the Watling-street, which keeps a straight direction to Ashby Ledgers, and Watford-gap, places particularly noticed by Stukeley, as leading to the next station of the Romans, called Tripontium, beyond Benavona—the other road leads to Birmingham and Coventry through Daventry.

Weedon Bec receives its name from a small religious house that was founded here as a cell to the abbey of Bec, in Normandy. It is evidently a place of great antiquity. Wulfere, one of the Kings of Mercia, had a palace here, and his daughter Werburgh, who was canonized as a saint, founded at this place a nunnery, which was endowed with singular privileges. This religious house, and probably the royal mansion, was burnt by the Danes. Leland says, that a chapel, dedicated to St. Werburgh, was existing in his time, attached to the south side of the church, which stands in the meadows, about a quarter of a mile from Weedon, and below the bed of the Grand Junction canal, which passes under the high London road, and is then carried over the valley by an embankment of earth, half a mile in length, and about 30 feet high. This embankment passing close to the Weedon church-yard, the top water-level is above the height of the body of the church, and nearly upon a parallel with the bells. As there is something novel and interesting in the place, we have introduced a view of it. The distant hills range in bold sweeping forms, the navigation reaching their brow, from an opposite direction, finds a permanent bed for its channel along their bases until it arrives at Stowe Hill. Two public highways for carriages, and a

Weedon Beck Church & Embankment across the valley.

small river, pass under the canal, through the base of
this embankment. At Weedon we come to the Roman
station called Benavona, or Benevenna. Camden, Bur-
ton, and Gale, all agree as to the station—but Stukeley
gives us the following account of it :—" the next station,
the Watling-street, leads us to Weedon-on-the-Street, beyond dispute *Benavona*, as surely it ought to be wrote,
being situate on the head of the Aufona, running to *North-
avanton*, or *Northamton ;* this too affords little matter
for the antiquarian. The old town seems to have been
in two pastures west of the road, and south of the church,
called Upper Ash Close, and Nether Ash Close, or the
Ashes, in which are manifest *vestiges* of the ditch and
rampart that surrounded it, and many marks of great
foundations. They shew you the scite of King Wulfere's palace. The *Saxon* kings of this province having
their seat here. The Ashes was the Roman castrum.
Here was a chapel of St. Werburgh, daughter of King
Wulfere, abbess to the nunnery of this place. An abundance of very fine stone, and many *Roman* coyns have
been dug up here. Weedon consists of two parishes, and
has been a *market* town. There is a large Roman camp
a little higher toward the river head, southward a mile,
as much from Watling-street, called Castle Dikes.; probably one of those made by P. Ostorius Scapula, proprætor under Claudius.

"Roman coyns and pavements have been found there.
The place is in a very pleasant and healthful situation,
being in a wood. Probably it was a Roman villa, after-
ward rendered Saxon. A house stands by it.

"Mr. Pennant thinks he finds a reason in the name for
placing the station at or near Borough Hill, immediately
adjacent to the town of Daventry. The Britons, he conjectures, would call this hill, as being near the source of

a river, according to their usual mode of giving appella-
tions to places: *pen* pronounced ben, and Avon, river,
i. e. *Ben-Avon*, or the head of the river. And as it is
well known the Romans latinized the British names, they
would naturally term it Benevenna, or as Stukeley
acutely observes, Benavona. This exactly answers to
the description of the place in question. One of the
rivers, Nen, has its rise near Daventry, and the ancient
name of this has been thought by most writers to have
been Aven or Avon.

" Horseley, whose opinion is also to be respected,
doubts whether to prefer Burrough Hill, or Ashby St.
Ledger, as Benavona. His reasons, he deduces from the
distances between this and the next station Venonis: in the
second iter the number of miles set opposite Benavona is
XV11. and this, he concludes, to be nearly accurate, from
the distance between Venonis and Benfavena, in the
eighth iter being set down XV l·II. which places, though
the names are somewhat different, he considers identi-
cally the same.

" I have therefore set off thirteen and a half computed
miles, according to the large scale in Camden, and find
it reaches exactly to Daventry, or Leger Ashby, or to
that part of Watling-street, that is over against those
places. The present town of Daventry stands to the
west of this great military way, but it is likely that the
ancient Roman town may have nearly come up to it."

There is sufficient evidence of a Roman station and
town at this part, as we shall shortly prove by our account
of Borough Hill, or as Stukeley calls it, *Burrow Hill.*

The latter part of the supposition of Horseley appears
to us to be extremely erroneous, for Daventry is only
four miles from the separation of the Watling-street at
Weedon; and upon the examination of any map lies only.

in a parallel line with Whilton Mill, on the Watling-
street; whereas Ledger Ashby is as far again. These
errors, which are continually occurring, arise from those
persons who foist on the public, compilations, in the
shape of county history, without having personally
visited a single spot they pretend to describe. The observations of Horsley, differing so materially from the
opinion of Stukeley, I endeavoured to make as close and
occular investigation of Benavona as the nature of the
place in the present day would admit; and I must, in
justice observe, that every spot Stukeley has pointed out,
bears a close affinity to what he records.

On the summit of the hill of Weedon Bec are the military buildings, called the *depôt*, which consists of a
governor's house and barracks, with storehouses for artil-
lery, muskets, cloathing, stabling for cavalry, &c. At the
lower part of the lawn, before the government-house, a cut
is made from the Grand Junction canal to the store houses ;
by this canal troops and stores can be readily conveyed
either to the metropolis or the northern counties. Beyond
Weedon, at a mile distance, is Dodford church, situated
on an eminence to the right, near a farm-house. It is a
very picturesque object, with a Gothic tower at the west
end. There are some monuments worthy of notice in
this church—one, a cross-legged knight in armour, with
both hands upon his sword, as if in the act of drawing
it. This effigy, it is presumed, is intended to represent
one of the Keymes, the ancient lords of the place, and
from the attitude of the legs, he is supposed to have lived
during the fashionable madness of the crusades. There
are two other personages interred here, William Wyde
and John Cressy, both men of some consequence.

The road continues through a pleasant country, and
on our left, at a considerable distance, is Fawsley, the

H

mansion of Sir Charles Knightley. This is a very ancient
seat of the Knightley family, and worthy of being visited
if time will permit. Some of the oldest parts are curious,
as calculated to display the customs and manners of our
baronial ancestors. The kitchens and hall are particularly entitled to notice ; the first, from their peculiar
fire-places; and the latter, for its lofty roof, window, and
ornamental chimney-piece. The kitchen is " most hospi-
tably divided ;" the chimney consists of two funnels, and
on each side of the partition is an enormous fire-place,
which are placed back to back, so as not to interrupt the
respective operations at each—one is 12 feet 6 inches,
and the other 14 feet 10 inches wide, with double-arched
mantle-pieces of stone. The hall, 52 feet in length, is
very lofty, and has a timbered roof, curiously carved.

The grand bow-window, forming the recess, is richly
ornamented with stone tracery and sculptured decora-
tions—the rest of the windows are very large, and placed
according to the fashion of the time, a considerable
height above the floor. In each are emblazoned, in
stained glass, the family arms, and those of the families
with which the Knightley's have been connected. The
chimney-piece is very curious, large, grand, admirably contrived, and richly decorated with tracery
mouldings; immediately over it is a handsome window. The smoke being conveyed through two fun-
nels, carried up inside the collateral buttresses of the fire-
place, preserves the uniformity of the hall as to the windows, as though it had no chimney. At the lower end
are two doors, in the pointed style. Among the pictures
are some respectable portraits of the Knightley family,
and others of eminent persons. The park is extensive,
and well stocked with deer.

Dr. John Wilkins, a celebrated divine and mathema-

tician, was a native of Fawsley. He lived in Cromwell's
time, and was a sort of Vicar of Bray, but a very eccen-
tric author. He gave the public, in 1638, a work, which
he styled " A Discovery of a New World in the Moon;"
or an attempt to demonstrate that there is another habi-
table world in that planet; in which he treats also of the
possible means of forming a communication with the
lunar inhabitants.

An excellent turnpike road, through a pleasant country,
with considerable eminences on each side, brought us to
Borrough, or Burrough Hill, known also by the name
of *Danes' Hill*, or Burrow Hill, according to Stukeley,
who gives the following account of it; but recommends
the antiquary to consult Morton's works, who has written
at large upon it. " I went out of the way (says Stukeley)
through Norton, to see a great camp, called Burrow Hill,
upon the north end of a hill, covered over with fern and
gorse. Here is a horse-race kept, and the whole hill-top,
which is of great extent, seems to have been fortified ;
but the principal work, upon the end of it, is a squarish
double ditch, of about 12 acres. The inner ditch is very
large, and at one corner has a spring. The vallum is
but moderate—a squarish work within, upon the highest
part of the camp, like a prætorium. They say this was
a Danish camp, and every thing hereabouts is attributed
to the Danes, because of the neighbouring Daventre,
which they suppose to be built by them. The road hereabouts too being overgrown with Dane-weed, they fancy
it sprung from the blood of the Danes slain in battle, and
that, if upon a certain day in the year you cut it, it
bleeds.

As to the camp, I believe it to be originally Roman,
but that it has been occupied by some other people, and
perhaps the Danes, who had new modelled the same, and

made new works to the former. Consult Mr. Morton,
who has discoursed very largely about it. Much *cotyledon*
and *ros solis* grow in the springs hereabouts; the stone
is red and sandy, and brim-full of shells. I saw a fine *cornu-
ammonis* lie neglected in Norton town road—too big to
bring away; and where they have fresh mended the Watling-street with this stone, 'twas an amusement for some
miles to view the shells in it. Hereabouts the road is
overgrown with grass and trefoil, being well nigh neglected, for badness, and the trade wholly turned another
way, by Coventry, for that reason. Between the head
of the Cam and the river Avon, Arbury Hill is in view,
another Roman camp, upon a very high hill, notoriously
made for a guard between the two rivers."

Morton, to whom Stukeley refers, minutely describes
the camp, and insists on its being originally three miles
in circumference; and supposing the area to be an oval,
being in the shape of an oblong, and resembling the human
foot, in which particular it assimilates to the most
formidable one the Romans had in the West of England,
called *Warle Berry*, in the county of Somerset. Presum-
ing the area to be two miles in circumference, it contains
no less than 190 acres. But the circuit is 10,560 paces,
and the length 587 paces of five feet to the pace; so,
allowing 9 feet square for the lodgment of every foot sol-
dier, no fewer than 99,700 soldiers might be quartered
here.

Near the northern extremity of the hill, the encampment was divided by a rampart, extending nearly across
the area from East to West—the part thus separated from
the larger fortifications, consisted of an area of about 12
acres. This is nearly of a circular form, and has at the
north-east end, an high mount, on which has been an *arx-
exploratoria*, or the prætorium of the general; and on the

east side of the foss is a spring, called Spelwell, which
Camden, by mistake, denominates a mound.

On the south-east side of the hill, about 300 yards from
the outer works of the larger encampment, is a smaller
camp, forming a parallelogram, or oblong square, encompassed by a single foss and vallum, having entrances
on the east and west sides.   The area includes about an
acre.

On the south, at the foot of the hill, is a remarkable
spot, denominated Burnt-Walls, where various walls,
arched vaults, foundations of buildings, &c. have been
discovered, and whence large quantities of stone have,
at different times, been removed, for the purposes of
building. The space these occupy, contains about six
acres, and appears to have formerly been surrounded
with a foss. Some antiquarians consider this was a moat,
and once supplied with water from the springs in Da-
ventry-park.

In a wood, contiguous to Burnt-Walls, are the vestiges
of some other fortified place, which is traditionally called
John of Gaunt's Castle, but it is doubtful if ever this
hero lived here, or possessed this post.   It was probably
part of the great Roman station at this place.

Mr. Pennant thinks the original encampment was the
work of the Britons, the nature of the construction agree-
ing with the description of the Gaulish and British mode
of fortifying places, left us by Tacitus.   " Tunc monti-
bus arduis & si qua elemantur accedi poterant in modum
valli saxa præstruit;" and the same author informs us,
that the Iceni took refuge from the army of the Roman
proprætor, Ostorius, locum pugna delegere, septum
agresti aggere et aditu Augusto, ne pemicus equis foret."
Tacitus Annal.—The Coritani, when assailed, would of
course avail themselves of such a strong position by na-

ture as this Borough Hill, and fortify it in a similar manner ; while Camden and others think it was the work of
the proprætor.

There can be little doubt but that Ostorious, took
possession of the strong holds, as he was victorious against
the natives of these parts, and finding this so eligible a spot to
make a stand, would as certainly new model and strengthen
the fortifications to increase it tenability, forming it into
a summer camp, and the warmer situation, beneath, into
an *hibernaculum*, or winter station. This he most probably established as a post, whilst traversing the island,
to quell the different risings of the insurgents. He fortified
the river Aufona or Nen, by which means the retreat of
Petilius Cerealis, the Roman general, was covered, after
his complete defeat by the Britons. On which occasion
the ninth legion was cut to pieces, nearly the whole of
his infantry either killed or taken, and he with difficulty
escaped hither, accompanied by a portion of his cavalry.

From these and other circumstances, antiquarians of
the first eminence have been induced to consider Borough
Hill, or rather Burnt-Walls, as the scite of a Roman
station.

Borough Hill appears to us to have been a place fixed
upon by the Romans as commanding a view of every inlet
upon their high roads, as is the case with this station ; it
is considerably above the steeple of Daventry church,
possessing an extensive view over the large reservoir
belonging to the Grand Junction, and all the surrounding
country, and every *debouchment* that an enemy might
make into the valley, or upon the Watling-street, would
be discernable from the Borough Hill's entrenchment.

I think Mr. Lysons makes a grand mistake in his
Magna Britania, in saying that the two Brick-hills at
Fenny-Stratford, stand upon the Watling-street. It is

true, that Roman road passes over the hill, on either
side of which stand Little Brickhill, but Great Brick-
hill is full a mile and a half to the westward of the former; and from the top of the hill, where Mr. Duncombe's
villa is, a complete command of all the open country
is to be had, which, from appearances, and its peculiar
situation, it is not unlikely might have been a small station of the Romans ; however that may be, Great Brick-
hill certainly does not stand upon the Watling-street.
Bow Brick-hill, which is three miles eastward of Little
Brick-hill, might also have been a small Roman station, as
it commands every part of the valley beneath it, and the
country all the way to Newport Pagnel. Here we cannot
but again regret, that Mr. Lysons, as a county historian,
has not attended to the geography of the county of Bucks,
of which he professes to give a history. We thought of introducing the view of the reservoir from Borough Hill
into our work, but finding it did not embrace the principal objects with sufficient compactness to make a good
composition, we deferred taking a view of this interesting
scene until we arrived at Daventry, where we purposed
resting ourselves for two days to arrange the materials
we had collected. " Daventry," says Mr. Pennant, " derives its appellation from the British words, Dwy—avon
tre, i. e. the town of the two Avons—synonimous with
a place situated between two rivers." It is a market
town, occupying the top and sides of a hill. The vulgar
notion received here is, that the place was originally
built by the Danes ; and from this ridiculous conceit the
costume of the town-crier has been taken, who bears on
his badge of office the effiges of a Dane cutting down a
tree, and thus it is interpreted Dane-tree.

Daventry, in the dooms-day book, appears a place of
some consequence. In the survey taken at the conquest,

the Norman William bestowed immense possessions here
on his niece, the Countess Judith, whom he had given in
marriage to Wattheof, the great Earl of Northumberland;
and to engage this nobleman's interest and fidelity,
granted with her in dower the county of Northampton,
and that of Huntingdon.   The earl afterwards engaged
in a conspiracy ; but repenting of the steps he had taken,
threw himself at the foot of the throne, and supplicated an
amnesty for himself and followers : but notwithstanding
such submission, he was beheaded in 1074, as it is said, at
the instigation of his wife.   This vicious woman, it appears,
had cast her adulterous eyes on another, whom she intended to marry ; but of this gratification she was disappointed by the policy of her uncle.   He introduced to
her choice a Norman nobleman, Simon de St. Liz, who
was lame.   Judith rejected him, which so enraged the
the king, that he alienated her honours and estates, and
granted them to St. Liz, on his marriage with the countess's daughter, leaving the mother to sigh in reluctant
widowhood.   A priory was founded at Daventry, in
1090, by Hugh de Leycester, for monks of the Cluniac
order, and subject to St. Mary de Caritate in Canterbury.
The number originally consisted of four only, who had
their habitation at Preston Copes.   Leycester was afterwards allowed to remove the establishment to Daventry,
where he erected a priory for them, near the parochial
church.   This house, by the long lists of grants and be-
nefactions, was most richly endowed, a circumstance
that did not escape the keen observations of Cardinal
Wolsey; for it was one of the monasteries dissolved by
permission of Pope Clement VII. and Henry VIII. in
the 7th year of his reign, and granted to the cardinal for
the purpose of erecting his intended new colleges of
Ipswich and Christ Church, in Oxford—but with what

Remains of the Cluniac Priory at Daventry.

Drawn by J. Edgell.

fatal consequences to the principal agents in this nefarious transaction, we are informed by Stowe, in his Annals.

Wolsey had excited five persons to provoke a dispute with the monks of this house, about the right of certain lands, and caused the same to be brought before him for a final hearing, as umpire in the cause. He embraced this opportunity of exercising the power, previously delegated by the pope and king, for dissolving the society, and seized on the revenues, on which Stowe thus remarks:

" But of this irreligious robbery, done of no conscience, but to patch up pride, which private wealth could not furnish, what punishment hath since ensued by God's hand, partly ourselves have seen ; for of those five persons, two fell at discord between themselves, and the one slew the other, for which the survivor was hanged ; the third drowned himself in a well ; the fourth, being well known, and valued worth £200, became in three days so poor, that he begged till his dying day ; and the fifth, called Dr. Allane, being chief executor of those doings, was cruelly maimed in Ireland, even at such a time as he was a bishop." The same author then proceeds to trace the hand of retributive justice to the cardinal, who died under Henry's displeasure—then to the colleges, one pulled down, and the other never completed by the patron—and finally, to the unrighteous pontiff, who was beseiged in his holy see, and subsequently suffered a long imprisonment by the Imperialists, who shut him up in the Castle of St. Angelo, at Rome. On the suppression of this priory, it was valued at £236 7s. 6d. The conventional was afterwards made the parochial church, which some years since was taken down, and a new edifice built. The monastery joined the west end of the old church, and thence the building extended northward ; the part yet remaining is supposed to have been the refectory,

and is one of the views that we have introduced, with its
ancient windows and door ways, some of them in the
pointed style, and a large flight of steps leading to the
apartments.

We visited the inside of the refectory, which is now
converted into a school, and found it destitute of every
thing but the forms and desks of the youths who are instructed in it. From its high antiquity, and being a
place so remarkable for the events attending it, we have
annexed two views—one simply as before described, the
west front—the other, the east front, with the church and
town. From the roof of the church we also made our
drawing of the grand reservoir, and the surrounding
country, in preference, as we before observed, to the
view from the Borough Hills. The annexed view looking down upon the lowest extremity of the church-yard,
whose wall takes a flowing line not unpictorial; beyond
which are the cottages which stands on the north-east
entrance of the town; a plantation of wood immediately fences and backs the houses from the vast
vacuum that the lake occupies; the hills on each side
of the reservoir range down to the water's edge, and the
distant view is terminated by a succession of woody
hills and eminences, rising above each other as far as the
eye can wander. This grand sheet of water occupies a
space of 130 acres, and by the means of its outlet and
sluices can give a sufficient supply of water to the Grand
Junction canal, until it reaches the bed of the river
Ouse. A branch of the river Ken or Can rises near Daventry, which passing in a north-east direction across the
navigation near Welton, forms itself with the more
northern stream, whence they take a southerly course to
the village of Flower, near to Weedon, and then pass
from that village to Northampton.

The large Reservoir at Daventry, Northamptonshire.

Daventry is a borough incorporated under a charter, said to have been originally granted by John. The town is governed by a bailiff, twelve burgesses, twenty common council men, usually called the " twenty men," a recorder, two serjeants at mace, and a town clerk.

William Parker, of London, a woollen draper, and a native of this place, founded a grammar school in 1576, and left an annual salary of £20 for a master, and £10 yearly to be distributed among six poor men. Five boys are educated by a legacy of Lord Crewe, formerly Bishop of Durham; and twelve others are supported at school at the expence of the corporation. There are five annual fairs held for the sale of horses. The market is held on a Wednesday; and by the returns made to parliament in 1801, the number of houses was five hundred and three, and inhabitants two thousand five hundred and eighty-two. It is celebrated for its manufacture of whips, horse harness, and shoes.

Daventry was the birth-place of Henry Holland, one of the translators of the Rhemish testament, a work of some notoriety, as being the subject of a long polemical controversy between the divines of the Catholic and Reformed churches; also of George Andrew, bishop of Fearns and Leighlin, in Ireland, who, on the breaking out of the Rebellion, was driven from his see, and died in London 1648. Mr. John Smith, a celebrated mezzotinto engraver, was also born here. In Walpole's Catalogue of Engravers, we find the following account of this artist: " The end of King William's reign was illustrated by a genius of singular merit in his way, John Smith, the son of John Smith, who had been three times bailiff of Daventry, and was placed out by his father as an apprentice to a painter in London, of the name of Tilley.

" When he had served the term, he applied to a Mr.

Becket, from whom he learned the art of engraving in
mezzotinto; and was further instructed by the famous
Van de Vaart. He then received admission into the
house of Sir Godfrey Kneller, to exercise his art in engraving the pictures of that eminent master. Besides
portraits, he also engraved a variety of historic and fancy
pieces, among which, the most admired, for its peculiar
delicacy of touch, is a holy family, after Carlo Maratti."

Previous to his death, Smith had collected proofs of
his various plates, in two large volumes. Walpole says,
" he was the best mezzotintor of the age; who united
softness with strength and finishing with freedom."
Smith died at Northampton, and was buried within the
precincts of St. Peter's church, where a tablet is raised
to his memory.

Daventry appears formerly to have been an ill built
town. The line of building, which stands upon the street
of the high thoroughfare, is very antique in parts, and
badly paved. The principal street is broad, spacious,
and well paved, though at the present time rather irregular
as to its buildings. The scite of it has the appearance
of a way that once led from the church to Burnt-Walls,
having a passage through the town by the side of the
Saracen's Head inn; or, perhaps, at the existence of the
monastery, it might be a mall from the friary to the town,
or else a favourite walk for the towns'-people.

We had now the gratification of knowing that nothing
of any import had been left unnoticed in our whole route,
and that the ensuing day would lead us to the pleasing
task of viewing the head of this interesting and picturesque
stream. We left Daventry, and an excellent inn for accommodation, the Saracen's Head, by the sun-rise, and
had a delightful view on our right of the reservoir, or
Daventry lake.

Daventry. — Northamptonshire.

It was a lovely morning in September, when

" Valley dews walk o'er the western hills."

All nature seemed alive, except a poor partridge, who, in crossing the road with wounds it had just before received from the shot of a sportsman, dropped dead from the covey it was flying with. We alighted, and having bagged our bird, anticipated a tolerable good supper.

The scenery on both sides of us was chearful and pleasant, and continued the same until we came to a full view of Braunston. On the summit of a hill, about a mile on the Daventry side of Little Braunston, an unbounded landscape opened to our view. The scenery towards the north, blended with the horizon, impressing the mind with an idea of infinity. Enveloped in all the lovely tints of morning, beauty gleamed on every hill.— Great Braunston lined the summit of the first distance— the protruding objects above the village—the church with a spire of 150 feet in height—a busy mill and some noble timber—broke the formality of the line, and gave a picturesque character to one of the sweetest scenes in nature. Little Braunston laying beneath the sight, as a bird's-eye view, intersected the line of the valley, and added an interest to the parts, which otherwise would have been less inviting. Nature does much in harmonizing her compositions, and on this morning she appeared to be in one of her happiest humours—the scene was characterized in a soft and delicate tone, and as the eye approached nearer towards the foreground, the pearls of dew were pendant, and glistening from every shrub and tree. Below the houses of Little Braunston, and through the openings of the trees, we have a glimpse of the reservoir of the Grand Junction, which is closed up by an abundance of wood that skirts the valley.

Lower Braunston stands most conveniently for the

accommodation of the navigation, and the persons having connection with it, and there is a respectable house for travellers.

The higher village, or Great Braunston, is situated on the borders of Warwickshire. The church is a noble structure, with an octangular spire, having crocketted angles, and elevated points of curious workmanship at each square of the tower. Near the upper end of the village is a stone-cross, composed of four diverging steps, on which is raised a shaft of an octagonal form, cut out of one block of stone, though eleven feet in height; and surmounted with a kind of emblature, decorated with four busts, supposed to be representative of the four evangelists. Conjectures are offered that it was erected for a land-mark by the convent of Nuneaton, which possessed two virgates of land in this parish. The tenure (according to Blount) of a considerable portion of this lordship being of a peculiar nature, is deserving of notice. If the widow of any copyholder appears in the manorial court, next ensuing the decease of her husband, and there presents a leathern purse, with a groat in it, she may become tenant, and hold his copyhold lands for life; but to render this tenancy valid, she must attend regularly every court-day.

Dr. Edward Reynolds, celebrated for his Calvinistic divinity, was at one time curate of this place. He presented the congratulatory address from the London ministers to Richard Cromwell, on his succeeding his father in the protectorship, and on that occasion was advanced to the see of Norwich, in 1661. The acceptance of a seat in the episcopal bench gave great offence to his former connexions. He died in 1676.

In the valley between the villages of Upper and Lower Braunston, the Grand Junction and Oxford canals unite

Head of the Grand Junction Canal with the small Reservoir at Braunston.

Drawn by I. Hassell

London Pub. 1. Oct. 1819. by I. Hassell, 15 Richard Street, Islington.

their streams. The Oxford canal is much more contracted, and dwindles into comparative insignificance
from being opposed to a navigation so much superior in
appearance at its junction—nevertheless, it is to the mother stream that the latter, in a great measure, has become
so estimable. By this canal all the manufactories of
Birmingham, Sheffield, Manchester, and the Potteries,
first enter the Grand Junction. It is to them that the
proprietors of this invaluable concern are so much
indebted for the large accumulation of their profits,
and the immense advance of their shares. Nor can we
with justice pass over their great undertakings without·
introducing the first great cause of these streams being
undertaken. Formerly the whole of the manufactories of
Birmingham were conveyed from that town by land
carriage. The expence attending the conveyance of
heavy goods induced the trade of Birmingham to pro-
cure the Coventry navigation, which, uniting with the
Oxfordshire canal, (one of the last undertakings of that
truly great man, Mr. Brindley,) they conveyed their
goods to Braunston by water, and from thence in
waggons to London.

The potteries of Staffordshire (a grand national monument of British industry,) found a peculiarly heavy
drawback upon their profits, arising from the immense expence of carriage of their articles. Situated in
a country abounding with coal, the most essential article
to the perfection of earthenware, they could in no instance think of removing from the certainty of an abundant supply, to a future precarious one, though perhaps
nearer the metropolis. The success with which the Duke
of Bridgewater's undertakings were crowned, encouraged
the manufacturers of Staffordshire to revive the idea of a
canal navigation through that country, for conveying

to market at a cheaper rate the products of Staffordshire.

This plan was patronised by Lord Gower and Mr.
Anson. Mr. Brindley was immediately engaged to make
a survey, when he reported it was practicable to construct
a canal to join the Trent and Mersey rivers, which united
a junction with the two out-ports of Hull to the eastward, and Liverpool to the west.

The late Mr. Josiah Wedgewood cut the first sod out
of this navigation, which the engineer emphatically styled
" The Grand Trunk Navigation." After this design was
determined upon, he completed the canal from Birmingham to the Grand Trunk; then came the Coventry canal
to unite those of Oxfordshire and Birmingham; and lastly,
though not least, was commenced the Grand Junction
canal, the very soul of trade, the *aorta ascendens et
descendens*, and the life, blood, and circulation of the
articles of our inland trade.

Some short account we shall here submit to our readers of the genius and enterprize of Staffordshire manufacturers, and then take our departure from the head of
the Grand Junction back to the capital, by a deviation
from our route downwards.

Stoke-upon-Trent is the parish town of the potteries,
and by far the greater part of the potteries are within its
boundaries. Stoke is situated about a mile and a half
to the east of Newcastle, on the river Trent, with the
Grand Trunk canal running parallel and passing through
the town.

The first pottery of consequence in this place is Mr.
Spode's manufactory of china and earthenware, and is
considered one of the most complete establishments of its
kind in the kingdom. Some idea may be formed of its
extent from the quantity of coal consumed, which is up-

wards of 200 tons per week, and from the number of ovens wherein the ware is baked, amounting to eighteen large furnaces, many of which are used three times each, weekly, the whole year round. There are about 800 people, of all ages, employed in this concern. The materials used in the manufactory are brought from a considerable distance; the clays from the counties of Dorset, Devon, and Cornwall, and the flint, principally from Kent. There are two steam-engines connected with the manufactory, the oldest of which has been erected nearly forty years; and the other, a most beautiful atmosphoric engine of 36 horse power was put up by Bolton and Watt, about ten years ago. These engines grind all the flints, glazes, colours, &c.; sift the liquid clay, or slip; compress the prepared clay into a more compact mass; and put in motion the throwing wheels and turning laths, which, in other factories is effected by pedal, and manual labour.

Here almost an endless variety of earthenware is made of every colour and fabric, and of a quality which has obtained for it an extended and merited celebrity.

China, too, has here been brought to the greatest perfection, both as regards its colour and transparency, and the taste displayed in its decoration. Here is also made the recently invented stone china, which is remarkably strong and durable, and in every respect much like the oriental; there is an immense quantity of it sold at present; and no doubt, but as it becomes better known, it will be introduced into very general use.

At Penkhull, is the Mount, the seat of Josiah Spode, esq.

The London concern of this manufactory is conducted by Mr. William Copeland, in Portugal-street; the show-rooms are a perfect exhibition, where numbers of nobility and gentry assemble daily, and have the gratification of

I

selecting their own services. The numerous wares resemble a picture gallery, where the exuberance of genius meets the sight in every direction. The advantage to the public is incalculable, by a dependence on receiving a sound article, and at a moderate price. To witness the variety, beauty, and extent of the produce of the manufacture, we would recommend a visit to this fashionable resort, where the greatest attention is paid to the company while inspecting the collection.

The celebrated Dr. Aikin received the following description of the process used in manufacturing the earthenware by a person on the spot, and the practice has varied very little since that time.

Process.—" A mixture of clay and ground flint, dried and prepared to a proper consistence, is taken to be formed into any required shape and fashion, by a man who sits over a machine, called a wheel; on the going round of which he continues forming the ware. This branch is termed *throwing ;* and as water is required to prevent the clay sticking to the hand, it is necessary for a short time to place it in a warmer situation. It then undergoes the operation of being turned, and is made much smoother than it was before ; by a person called a *turner;* when it is ready for the handle and spout to be joined to it, by the branch called *handling.* Dishes, plates, tureens, and many other articles, are made from moulds of ground plaster ; and when finished, the whole are placed carefully in saggars,* and taken to the oven. The ware, when removed from the oven, is called *biscuit,* and the body of it has much the appearance of a new tobacco-pipe, not having the least gloss upon it. It is

---

* Saggars is a corruption of the German, "Schragers," which signifies cases or supporters, in which the wares are burnt.

then immersed or dipped into a fluid, generally consisting of sixty pounds of white lead, ten pounds of ground
flint, and twenty pounds of stone from Cornwall, burned
or ground, all mixed together, and as much water put
to it as reduces it to the thickness of cream, which it
resembles. Each piece of ware being separately immersed or dipped into this fluid, so much of it adheres
all over the piece, that when put into other saggars, and
exposed to an operation of fire, performed in the
glossing kiln or oven, the ware becomes finished by ac-
quiring its glossy covering, which is given it by the
vitrification of the above ingredients. Enamelled ware
undergoes a third fire, after its being painted, in order to
bind the colour on.

A single piece of ware, such as a common enamelled
tea pot, a mug, jug, &c. passes through, at least, fourteen
different hands, before it is finished ; viz. the slip-maker,
who makes the clay ; the temperer, or beater of the clay ;
the thrower, who forms the ware ; the ball-maker and
carrier ; the attender upon the drying of it ; the turner,
who does away its roughness ; the spout-maker ; and the
handler, who puts to the handle and spout. The first, or
biscuit fireman, the person who commences or dips it
into the lead fluid ; the second, or glass fireman ; the
dresser, or sorter, in the warehouse ; the enameller or
painter ; the muffle, or enamel fireman. Several more
are required to the completion of such pieces of ware,
but are in inferior capacities, such as turners of the
wheel, turners of the lath, &c."

The extent of our excursion, terminating with the junction of the Braunston canal, with that of Oxfordshire,
at this spot, we turned our horses on the tow-path, and
passed over a stream from the Oxford canal that leads
up to the wharfs and warehouses, the property of the

proprietors of that concern, and we have here a complete view of the small reservoir at the head of the Braunston navigation. It lies on our right, in an extensive double sheet of water, connecting both pools by a passage under a single arched bridge, of the same character as those over the canal. (The tow-path dividing the reservoir, and the Grand Junction.) On our left is the barge steram of the navigation, which runs in a parallel line with the reservoirs. The scenery is very interesting, and rather singular —at the second arch, where the weighing engine on one side, and a lock-house on the other, are backed by a noble wood that ranges down the brow of the hill, and is met by another, of less consequence on the opposite side of the canal. In the centre of this view, and on the first rising ground, a steam-engine is seen, which acts in a double capacity; either supplying the navigation with what additional water it may want—or, on the contrary, taking any superfluous supply it no longer stands in need of, and returning it into the reservoir below. From under the arch of the bridge, another interesting view is presented, composed of the same materials as the scene just described; but the navigation, from not being contracted, has a bolder appearance. The back ground is just the same character as the former view.

Passing by the tow-path, through the next bridge, we are presented with the weighing-house, where all the boats that navigate the canal, go under its shed to have their tonnage ascertained. At an hundred yards distance beyond the lock-house, on turning round, and looking towards Braunston,—the steam-engine is seen now close at hand on the left, while the bridge, lock, and the other objects, make up a pretty scene. Continuing along the horse-road, by again turning ourselves round, at the level of the last lock, before reaching the tunnel, we

Loch descending North of the entrance of the Braunston Tunnell.

Drawn by I. Hassell.

have still a more interesting landscape: the scenery
is richly wooded, and the objects more diversified.
The level of the canal is suddenly interrupted by a considerable fall, and this continues, occasionally, all the
way we came from Braunston; though only one mile
from the tunnel entrance to that village. The water
is raised to pass on a level through that excavation,
37 feet by lockage, with depth of water for vessels of 60
tons burthen. From the valley to the tunnel, there are
seven locks; each of which are usually passed in three
minutes, whilst many of those, from Leighton to London,
occupy seven minutes in the same operation.

The entrance to the Braunston tunnel very much
resembles the one we have described at Stoke Bruerne,
excepting that the latter has more wood about it; consequently, a better general scene and more picturesque.

We rise over the Tunnel Hill, by a gradual ascent,
until we reach Mickle Moor House, which stands near
the turnpike road that leads from Daventry to Kilsby,
over the Braunston tunnel. At this elevation we have
a charming view of Daventry and Burough Hills, in the
distance, and the large reservoir intervening between us
and those places; and on its banks are fruitful pasturage
and rich woods. There are a multitude of sketches
and select bits, for the port-folio of an artist around
these parts; and the cottages are remarkable picturesque. Towards Ledger Ashby and Watford-gap, there
is a vale, or level meadow, of considerable extent.
We regretted our time did not allow us to visit it, for
Stukeley has given such a fascinating picture of its
beauties, that nothing short of our tour being limited, pre-
vented us. He says, " the ridge of hill, which the
Watling-street passes on, continues for miles, the nature
of the way on both sides being stony, has spared it.

Several *tumuli* upon the road, and *bodys* found under them, shows the *Romans* did not travel upon them on horse-back. Ledger Ashby, near here, has been another old town, as they say, destroyed by the Danes; there are great ditches, causey's, and marks of streets. The cele-brated Catesby, who hatched the powder-plot, owned the town. It is a most curious circumstance, that the ancestor of Robert Catesby, who held the manor of Ashby, viz. John de Catesby, was a commissioner from the crown for suppressing unlawful assemblies during the famous insurrection under Jack Straw and Wat Tyler, in the reign of Richard II. Robert Catesby ren-dered himself notorious by having been the projector of the powder-plot conspiracy. A small room in the detached offices, belonging to the manorial house, is still shown as the council-chamber of the conspirators. Catesby, for this inhuman design, was beheaded; and his head, with that of his father-in-law, Thomas Percie, another of the con-spirators, was fixed on the top of the parliament-house."

At a mile and a half distance, we come to the termi-nation of the tunnel, at Welton. The time a loaded barge takes, to push through this excavation is nearly an hour and a half; an unloaded boat, will do it in an hour.

At Welton, the Grand Junction company have a resi-dent engineer (Mr. Thompson) a gentleman of consi-derable talent and experience. His business is to super-intend, and to survey the works, bridges, and roads; to preserve the water belonging to the navigation; to regulate the outlet from the reservoirs; to report all repairs required; and to keep the canal in a navigable state.

Continuing the tow-path for some distance, we reach the junction of the Grand Union and Union canals at

Thorpe-lodges. These navigations lead away in a northerly direction to Leicester and Nottinghamshire. Here we come once more upon the Watling-street, and return immediately southward, keeping the navigation and some charming scenery on our left; and then continue our course to Norton, from thence to Brock-hall, the seat of Thomas Reeves Thornton, esq. A pleasant ride brought us back again to Weedon. While our dinner was preparing, we visited Flower, called, in Doomsday-Book, Flora; in all probability from its delightful situation. The church was given, in the reign of King John, to Merton Abbey, in Surrey; at the dissolution, it was granted to Christ Church, Oxford; to which college it now belongs. Here is a brass plate, with figures of the Virgin and Child; and Thomas Knaresburgh, in armour, with Agnes his wife. He died in 1450, and she, in 1483.

A cheerless rainy afternoon succeeded one of the finest autumn mornings; and as we had determined on sleeping that night at Northampton, we prepared for the storm, and enjoyed the united comforts of a *delectable* shower-bath, a bad road, and a most unpleasant ride; and, until within two miles distance of that town, we had little opportunity to make any remarks on the scenery.

Here suddenly the clouds dispersed, and the setting-sun shone in its brightest splendor, whilst, to add grandeur to the effect, one of the most vividly coloured rainbows, backed by the dark clouded curtain of evening, formed a scene, at once grand and beautiful, beyond description. Northampton, with its bright churches, appeared illuminated; the valley was partially touched with sun-beams and shadow; the russet face of nature, which had just before been bedewed with copious showers, was seen in the finest tones of colouring, heightened, and brought majestically to the view, by deep

shaded woods. For the compass of miles every thing
appeared in harmony—the rainbow that had shewn a
few minutes since, in its varied coloured densities, now
began to refract; and changing its determination, incur-
vated to a second reflection, and again altered its rays
to a third vision of colour. I had often before seen a
doubly radiated bow, but never, until the present moment,
beheld so grand, so glorious, and I may add, so divine
a composition.

Algerotti, on the nature of colours, in adducing his
prismatic representations of the rainbow, was but faint in
comparison with the awful scene before us; yet such are
his researches, that he delights, and informs, his readers.
Chance, one day, gave me an opportunity of ascertaining,
that colours are produced by a rapidity of motion. I
was on a fishing party, under the shade of some tall elms,
in the garden of Lord Henry Fitzgerald, at Thames
Ditton, when my eye was diverted from the float, by a
repetition of reflections in the water, resembling a rainbow; and on casting my eyes to observe the cause, I perceived an idle servant wench, gaping, occasionally, at
our party; and then lowering a mop into the water,
she had brought to wash, which, when fully saturated,
she drew up, and began trundling on her arm with velo-
city. From the emanation of the fluid, and the rapidity
of the motion, and that in the full meridian of the sun, I
observed it formed the three primary colours, to an ex-
actness I had never before seen, but by the rainbow—
the difference between the mop and the grand arch was,
that the last only forms a radius, while the mop produced
a complete circle of colours.

Northampton.—We entered this town at an inaus-
picious hour, just the evening before the races; but the
attention and civility of the master of the George inn,

gave us little occasion to complain. There is some gratification in knowing, that the house you may select for
accommodation, gives bread and education to the poor.
The George inn was given by John Dryden, esq. of
Chesterton, for the maintenance of the blue-coat school,
which he established here about the year 1710. The
trustees appointed to superintend the charity, obtained
an act of parliament to sell this house, and invest the
money in the funds, for the benefit of that institution. The
George inn was purchased by a society of persons, who
subscribed £50 each, and is now their property. A
town where races are held, and on the evening before
the sports begin, may justly be compared to the workmen of the Tower of Babel—the jargon of different
provincial countrymen—mountebanks and showmen—
hawkers, jockies, and black-legs—dandies, and fine ladies
—make up a motley group; while confusion, noise, and
uncomfortableness, are the only pleasure a non-admirer
of such amusement can expect. Northampton consists of
two principal streets, running north and south, and east
and west; intersecting each other about midway, and each
street nearly a mile in length. Most of the houses are built
of a reddish coloured sand stone, dug from quarries in the
neighbourhood. There are some brick buildings, and
others of a yellowish stone. At the eastern extremity of the
town, is a pleasant walk, called the New Walk, or Vigo Para-
dise Walk, and was made at the expense of the corporation.

At the farthest extremity, is a spring of chalybeate
water, inclosed with steps and walls, and near the upper
end, is another spring of clear water, known by the name
of *Thomas-à-Becket's Well.* At the north side of the
town, is a tract of land, which, in the year 1778, was an
open field of 894 acres; but in that year, an act was obtained to inclose it; about 129 acres of this was allotted·

to the freemen of the town for cattle, &c.: but it was
provided, in the act, that the same may be claimed and
used as a race-course, for any two days, between the
20th of July and the 20th of October.

There are four parish churches remaining, out of seven;
the number formerly existing. These are, St. Peter's;
St. Sepulchre's; St. Giles's; and All Saints'. St. Peter's
church stands in the vicinity of the castle, at the western
extremity of the town. The advowson was given by
Edward III. to the masters, brethren, and sisters of
St. Catherine's hospital, near the Tower, London, with
whom it has ever since continued. It was the privilege of
this church, that a person accused of any crime, intend-
ing to clear himself by canonical purgation, should do it
here, and in no other place of the town, having first performed his vigil and prayers in the said church, the evening before. Hence it appears, according to Bridges, that
this church was invested with the privilege of sanctuary,
and it may also be inferred, that it was founded by, or
under the patronage of, some powerful person or society.

The architecture of St. Peter's church is curious, and,
in many particulars, it may be considered unique; but
there is no record of its erection.

It is presumed, by the most learned antiquaries, to have
been built about 50 years after the Norman conquest.
It consists of a nave and two aisles of equal length,
having seven columns on each side; all the capitals are
charged with sculpture of scroll-work, heads, animals,
&c. The most curious part of the interior of this beautiful
structure, is the great archway beneath the tower, at the
western end of the nave; this consists of three receding
arches, each charged both in elevation and soffit, with
zig-zag mouldings. On each side of the archway, are
three pilaster columns; some of which are ornamented

spiral and lozenge mouldings.   The exterior of the church and tower is equally curious.

At the south-west, and north-west angles of the tower, are buttresses of peculiar form, each consisting of three semi-columns gradually diminishing at every story. On the north and south sides of the same, are two series of arcades; and at the west end one range corresponding, with a blank arch, having three rows of flat stones charged with varied tracery in pannels; at the south side is an ancient door way with a semi-circular arch.

The front, erected about the time of Edward I. is covered with blank arches, crocketted pediments, &c. This elegant building is still in high preservation, and it is to be hoped (that the present monstrous taste of beautifying and embellishing with plaster and white wash,) that some of our best and choicest specimens of antiquity, may be averted from meeting the fate of the relics of St. Peter; and may those unhallowed hands that cause it, be denied the entrance to that place of which the saint, it is said, possesses the keys.

It is very singular, in the present age of refinement, that we should not be able to preserve those beautiful relics that our forefathers have, with some care, handed down to us. Is it not barbarous that when a parochial job shall be wanted, that the churchwardens and over-seers, can cause a mutilation of the noblest fragments of antiquity, that a draper, grocer, or butcher, shall, in an official capcaity, nod assent to the devastion of the noblest works of art? It is a disgrace to the gentlemen of Britain, who look on calmly, and view the dilapidations of these modern Goths, without applying to the fountain-head, the legislature, to appoint proper antiquarian surveyors who should decide on the method of repair, and preservation of our still remaining vestiges of the rarest workmanship. The pillage that has taken place of stained glass, from the windows of our churches, is a disgrace to those clergy who have held the benefice at such times. The sums of money that of late years have been made in this sort of sacrilegious traffic, is beyond the general belief.

St. Sepulchre's church is presumed, by Mr. Pennant, and some other antiquarian writers, to have been "built by the Knights Templers, on the model of that at Jerusalem." This circumstance arises from its affinity with the churches of the Temple, (London) Little Maplestead, Essex, and that of the Holy Sepulchre at Cambridge; all of which, as well as St. Sepulchre, are round buildings. St. Sepulchre's church is situated near the northern extremity of Northampton.

St. Giles's church is situated at the eastern end of the town, and All Saint's about the centre of it. At the west end of this church, a tablet records the name of John Bailes, who was born in this town, and lived to a very advanced age. He existed in three centuries. Bridges observes, that " his age appears to have been assigned conjecturally to 126." He was at most but 114 years old ; he was a button-maker, and attended all the neighbouring markets and fairs, to dispose of his own manufactory. At the south-west corner of this church-yard is a conduit, covered with a small octangular building, which was formerly ornamented with eight pinnacles, and tracery, in two rows of pannels.

Northampton returns two members to parliament ever since the 12th year of Edward I. when it sent two members to represent that borough at Acton Burnet, in Gloucestershire, where the parliament was then held. It is considered an open borough, the right of voting being invested in every householder paying scot and lot. The number of voters are about 1000. The memorable election in 1768, was nearly the ruin of three noblemen, who opposed each other's interest, and had it been the final annihilation of them, for committing the grossest violation of our constitution, by daring to attack the sacred rights of elective franchise, they would have deserved it—

The Earls, Halifax, Northampton, and Spencer, were opposed to each other. Never, perhaps, was bribery so extensively and lavishly employed, and though all the parties were not positively ruined, yet each was materially injured in fortune. It is stated that Lord Spencer expended £100,000; and each of the other noblemen £150,000.

It is probable that it was Simon de Liz, who married the niece of William the Norman, that erected the castle at Northampton, as the delegation of his title as Earl of Northampton, and the conveyance of the lands of that county to him, was a considerable time after the making up of Doomsday-Book ; and this is very easily accounted for, by observing, that De Liz was married to the daughter of the great Earl of Northumberland, which might have been a period of seventeen to twenty years subsequent to the survey made at the time of the Conquest. However this might be, its building is attributed to that nobleman. In Henry II. it was possessed by the crown. In the civil war between Henry III. and his nobles, we find it in possession of the confederate barons, under the banner of the Earl of Leicester, whose son, Simon de Montford, was then its governor. The king, having received considerable reinforcements from the northern barons, his adherents besieged the castle with great vigour ; but the admirable situation and strength of the fortress, with the undaunted courage of the garrison, composed of the finest troops of the earl, under the direction of officers of distinction, famed for their skill and valour, baffled all the efforts of the royal troops, and convinced them that force was totally inadequate to their arduous enterprize. At length, recourse was had to a stratagem, not altogether just or manly in principle, but which effectually served their purpose. While the barons were engaged in a parley, under pretence of negociation, a chosen body of the royal forces was dispatched to make a breach in the walls at the opposite extremity of the town; the plan succeeded. The garrison thus taken by surprize, were, notwithstanding a brilliant display of courage, completely overcome, and surrendered themselves prisoners of war. In 1662, pursuant to an order of the council, the walls and gates, and part of the castle, were demolished, and the scite of it soon afterwards sold to Robert Haselrig, esq. in whose family it continues. By an inquisition, taken in the time of Edward I. it appears that the town walls were embattled, and at different places had steps to ascend them; like the walls round the city of Chester, they served for a public walk; they also constituted the best foot-path in winter, from one extremity of the town to another. This walk is reported to be wide enough for six persons to walk abreast. Leland mentions the walls and gates standing when he visited it.

The events that have happened in Northampton, its political and local history, and its immense strength as a fortified town, renders it an object of peculiar notice. Of whatever it might have been, in the time of the Danes, we have but little record.

The period of which it first appears of any consequence was in the year 1064, when the Northumbrians, under Earl Morcar, took possession of it; who, in the savage manner of their time, burned the houses, and murdered the male inhabitants, carrying away thousands of cattle, and multitudes of female prisoners.

When the celebrated statutes of Clarendon were established in Henry the Second's reign, for the good order of the kingdom, and for the better defining the boundaries of ecclesiastical jurisdiction, and Archbishop Becket alone refused his assent, which eventually proved fatal to him, a council of the states was convened at Northampton, before whom the archbishop was summoned to appear and answer the charges of contumacy, perjury, &c. which then should be exhibited against him.

In the 26th year of that monarch's reign, a convention of the barons and prelates was assembled here, to amend, confirm, and enforce the constitutions of Clarendon. By this council the kingdom was divided into six circuits, and justices were assigned to each. From the formation of this convention, the advice of the knights and burgesses being required, as well as that of the nobles and prelates, it has been considered as the model by which parliaments have been constituted in succeeding times ; the King of Scotland, with the bishops and abbots of that kingdom, attended this council to profess their subjection to the church of England. It appears a mint was established here in the 10th Richard I. when Geoffrey Fitzwalter paid 40s. to be discharged from the inspection of the mint. Had he lived at the present time, it is probable he would have given a thousand times that sum to have been appointed to it.

On the death of King Richard, John, his successor, being then in Normandy, a great council of the nobles assembled in Northampton, and were prevailed upon by the adherents of the new monarch to take an oath of fealty, and support his claim to the crown. King John, in the 10th year of his reign, having been displeased with the citizens of London, commanded the exchequer to be removed to Northampton. In the 13th year of his reign, a council of lay nobles was convened here; the king met the pope's nuncio's, Pandulph and Durand, in order to adjust those differences which had long subsisted between him and the holy see. The king made large concessions; but as he would not, or could not, restore to the clergy their confiscated effects, the treaty was broken off, and the king was solemnly excommunicated by the legates. During the reign of Henry III. the town was highly favored by that monarch, and in the war between that king and the confederate barons, it was alternately besieged and possessed by each of the contending parties. The students of Oxford and Cambridge formed a new seminary here at this period; but, taking side with the barons, they were dispersed by a royal mandate, which compelled those legislating youths to return to their old seminaries.

In the 7th year of Edward I. a most atrocious act was committed by the Jews residing in Northampton—they crucified a Christian boy, who fortunately survived their cruelty. For this diabolical act fifty of them were drawn at horses' tails, and publicly hanged; in the preceding year 300 of them had been hanged for clipping the coin. These and other enormities rendered the Jews so odious, that in the eighteenth year of this reign, a statute was passed for their total expulsion from the kingdom, and for the confiscation of their property. Another parliament was held here in 1317, in which an impostor, of the name of John Paydras, son of a tanner at Exeter, was brought to trial for affirming he was the real son of Edward I. and that the King was a carter's son, and substituted at nurse in his stead; producing no evidence however, in support of his assertions, he was condemned, and executed.

The last parliament that was assembled here, was the 4th of Richard II. when the poll-tax was levied, which occasioned the rebellion, wherein Wat Tyler was the chief.

The next memorable event that distinguished this place was the decisive battle fought in its vicinity between the York and the Lancasterian parties, in the 38th year of Henry VI. when that imbecile monarch was made prisoner. We find it favoured with a visit by Elizabeth, in 1563, and by Charles I. in 1634. It was ravaged by the plague in 1637; and in 1642, was seized by the parliamentary forces, by whom it was fortified. It has suffered repeatedly from fire, but the most melancholy occurrence of this nature happened in the year 1675, when the greater part of the town was consumed, and many of the poor inhabitants reduced to great distress; above 600 dwelling-houses were then burnt, and more than 800 families deprived of their habitations and property. The city of London set their usual example of benevolence, and subscribed £5,000, for the poor sufferers—a sum of money of no small consequence in those days. Mr. Pennant asserts, that £25,000 were collected by briefs and private charity, and the king gave 1000 tons of timber (we should presume loads) out of the Whittlebury forest, and remitted the duty of chimney-money, for seven years. It may be curious to remark, that the general subscription raised on account of the memorable fire of London did not exceed £18,000.

As the races were likely to afford us but little sport and novelty, we took our leave of Northampton by sunrise, and were saluted by another lovely morning. The valley between this town and Gayton is one entire collection of variegated beauty, with the navigation sweeping through its expanse in a double curve. From this

K

last village we continued in a straight line until we arrived at Forster's-booth, a pleasant spot on the Watling-street; the road now led insipidly over hill after hill without any thing like the character of a prolific country, but more resembling new-made inclosures, and at ten miles distance from Northampton, and four from Forster's-booth, we reach Towcester. Most of the antiquarians have differed about the station of Lactorodum. Horsley places it here, while Stukeley affirms it to have been at Stony Stratford, which appears more likely, if Benevona was actually at Weedon Bec. Now, as Towcester is little better than six miles from Weedon, and about the same distance from Stony Stratford, we have here the proper measurement according to the Itinerary.

How Towcester could be a station, I am at a loss to conjecture, unless Horsley means to infer, that Daventry was the Benevona between Lactorodum and Tripontium; and how could this be? for Daventry lies off the Watling-street five miles westward in every direction. This circumstance refutes the conjecture, as Tripontium being placed at Dovebridge-on-the-Avon, exactly corresponds with the proper Roman measurement to Benevona.

Towcester has undoubtedly been a place of considerable notoriety as far back as the time of the Danes, for we find the Danish soldiers occupying Northampton and Leicester, who had previously made a truce with the Saxons, suddenly breaking their league, marched upon this place, carrying on an assault for a whole day; the forces barely resisted the attack, and the Saxon army arriving in time for succour, the Danes were compelled to retreat. This caused King Edward, A. D. 921, towards the autumn of that year, to advance his army to Passenham, a village near Stony Stratford, until he had

fortified Towcester, and encompassed it with a stone
wall. Towcester is one long street, and near its centre
is a wide open space, where the market is held. In this
part of the town there is a remarkable elegant draper's
shop, said to be the largest in England, kept by Mrs,
Jenkinson; it is 20 yards long by 8 yards wide, and 12
feet high; she has two other warehouses of the same
length in the same house; and at the farther end, near
the church, is the mansion of Gilbert Fletcher, esq. a
gentleman of infinite taste in the fine arts, and possessing
an excellent collection of pictures. The White Horse
inn, in Towcester, affords as comfortable quarters as any
traveller would wish to find. William Sponne, archdea-
con of Norfolk, and rector of Towcester, gave the Talbot
inn, to pay a tax then in contemplation, called the *fif-
teenths*, if it should be levied by parliament, and in case
no such tax should take place, then the revenue to be
applied by the feoffees, for repairing and paving the
streets of the town. He also founded here a college and
chantry, for two priests to pray for his soul, and the
souls of his relations; the revenues of which, at the Dissolution, were valued at £19 6s. 8d. per annum. A
monument in the church commemorates this benefactor
to the town. Silk and lace are the principal manufacture of this place, and the adjoining villages. The town
is situated in a valley, and has the small river Tove passing near it. The most remarkable place in its neighbourhood is *Berry-mount-hill*, which is an artificial
mount, composed of earth and gravel, on the north-east
side of the town; it is a flat on the top, about 24 feet in
heighth, and the diameter 102. This hill was surrounded
by a moat, capable of being filled with water from the
adjoining brook. Many Roman coins have been found
in the neighbourhood. Here was born that noto-

rious villain, Sir Richard Empson, the associate of the infamous Dudley ; he was the son of a sieve maker of this place. By his assiduity as an attorney, he became well skilled in the law, and eminent as a favourite to the then pusillanimous monarch, Henry VII. who made him chancellor of the duchy of Lancaster, and to serve the purposes of royal avarice, elevated him to the post of enforcer and collector of the penal statutes throughout the kingdom ; his companion, Edmund Dudley and himself were so rigidly severe that they incensed all classes of the community, and at length became so obnoxious, that the tyrant, Henry VIII. was so beset with complaints and clamours from every description of persons, that he was constrained to bring them to trial, and sign his hand for their execution. Empson was beheaded at Northampton, August 16, 1510. The conduct of Henry VII. shews how little feeling monarchs have towards their subjects, even though, like him, they should so long have suffered in adversity. This king's vile ingratitude to his people was only surpassed, perhaps, by his avarice.

The country beyond Towcester becomes more interesting and woody ; at nearly two miles distance beyond that town, we pass Easton Neston, the seat of Lord Pomfret, a mansion of no small importance, situate among woods, with the fine rising country of Stoke Bruerne, Plane Woods, and Blisworth, beyond it, in the distance. It is said to have been partly built by Sir Christopher Wren, and partly by Hawkesmoor; but since that time it has been considerably altered.

A singular anecdote is related of Mr. Richard Fermor, who lies interred in the church at this place. He invited a number of his friends and relatives, of whom, after having taken a serious and affecting leave, he retired to his closet, and was found dead in the act of devotion.

The seat of Lord Pomfret was once enriched with an elegant collection of pictures, busts, &c. the works of the most eminent artists, which Henrietta Louisa, Countess of Pomfret, presented to the University of Oxford in 1755.

A storm, which had been some time gathering over the country towards Northampton, now approached the distant hills of Blisworth and Stoke Bruerne, communicating a most beautiful deep purple tone to the rich scenery around them, and combining the whole into a grand effect. The broken ground on which we were standing, and the objects on a small heath before us, made as desirable a composition for a picture as ever came from the pencil of Morland or Gaiusborough, both of whom were true copyists of this peculiar description of scenery. The storm increasing, we were driven for shelter to the village at Cuttle Mill, a very pretty rural spot.

On the brow of a hill beyond this, on our right, we pass the entrance into Whittlebury forest, which is part of the honour of Grafton; a perambulation made in the reign of Edward I. describes separately the parts lying within the three before-mentioned counties. The bounds of the forest, and the operation of the forest laws, were greatly extended by 15 Charles I. but an act of parliament in the next year restored the ancient limits as prescribed by the perambulation of Edward I. a part only of the lands within these limits, seems now to be considered as forest ; that part contains 5424 acres, and is almost encircled with a ring mound, which has been its boundary within the memory of the oldest man ; the rest of the land, without the mound, and within the perambulation, consists of many estates belonging to several proprietors, who are, in some instances, entirely, and in others, partially exempt from the forest laws.

The whole is divided into five walks, viz. Hazleborough, Sholbrook, Wakefield, Hanger, and Shrobb. The coppices in this forest are cut in rotation at 21 years growth; after each cutting, they are inclosed for 9 years, and then thrown open to the deer and cattle for the remaining 12. The wood, underwood, and timber, in seven coppices, being that part of Hazleborough walk, now belong to Earl Bathurst; the Crown having no other right than that of herbage, and cover for the deer; the remaining 62 coppices belonged to, and were in the actual possession of the Crown till 17 Charles II. when this forest, and that of Salcey, were settled on Queen Catherine for life, as part of her jointure. In the 25th year of the same reign, the coppices in both forests were granted to Lord Arlington, for his life, after the queen's death, with remainder to the Duke of Grafton, and other sons of the king. This forest is under the superintendance and care of a lord warden or master forester, lieutenant or deputy warden, two verderers, woodward, purliew ranger, five keepers, and six page keepers, besides the surveyor-general of the woods and forests.

By a grant of 2d Anne, the Duke of Grafton holds the office of lord warden or master forester, which gives him possession of the chief lodge, called Wakefield-lodge, with its appurtenances, containing about 117 acres, with pasturage for cattle in common with the deer.

His Grace has also, as hereditary keeper, the custody and management of the deer. No more, however, seems to have been required from his family, since the date of the patent, than to answer certain warrants for the supply of his majesty's household, and the demands of those accustomed to have venison from the royal forests. The number of deer said to be usually kept within the forest is about 1800, of all sorts; and the number killed one

year with another is 140 bucks and 100 does. In the
survey made in 1608, upwards of 200 years since, Whittlebury forest was said to contain 51,046 timber trees of
oak ; by the survey taken in 1783 there appeared to be
growing in this forest 5,211 timber trees fit for the navy,
containing 7,230 loads of timber (square measure) and
402 scrubbed, dotard, and decayed trees, containing 569
loads. The same survey states that there were 18,617
trees in the forest constantly lopped for browse for the
deer, viz. 6335 oak trees, computed to contain 8,907 loads
of timber (square measure) being more than a load and
a quarter each tree, on an average, and 12,282 ash trees,
containing 3,512 loads ; so that the number and contents
of the browsed oaks was greater than of the oak trees
reported to be fit for the navy, of which the number in
the coppices was not quite three trees to every two acres
of land. Between the years 1772 and 1783 there had
been felled for the navy 1,461 trees, producing 1335 loads.
If there be added to the trees of thirty feet and upwards,
growing in the coppices at the time of the survey, the
number would still be less than two trees to an acre ;
and if the browse oaks be taken into the computation,
the whole number of the trees of thirty feet in height and
upwards would be little more than three trees to an acre.
Excepting the persons immediately connected with the
forest, little benefit arises in a general way to the public,
and what ought, in a national view, to be highly beneficial to the country, is contumaciously treated, and the
public scoffed at. Self aggrandizement is substituted for
the *amor patriæ*, and robbery is the political watch-
word of a dignified banditti. A celebrated chief justice
of Ireland some short time since observed, " it did the
state more service to hang one rascal in ruffles than fifty
raggamuffins." If the experiment were tried upon a

number of timber plunderers, the navy of Great Britain might always command a few oaks for its repairs. This species of tree thrives well in our soil, and nature appears to have given us, as an island, the means of growing our defensive bulwark, the navy ; but if rats are to devour our protection, farewell, one time or other, to the power of resistance. The worst of effects in forests arise from the destruction of young timber, by lopping them for browse wood, and from peculation by the officers entrusted with the care of them, who are enriched at the public expence. Some years since, a committee of the House of Commons made the following report to the legislature, and recommended the means for the preservation of this valuable national property, but, like many other wholesome regulations, it has fallen back into the stew of corruption.

Report.—" The office, or commission of surveyor of the woods, as at present constituted, the nature of its perquisites, and the mode of executing the business of that department, are additional causes of waste and expence. The poundage of 5 per cent. on all monies coming to the hands of the surveyor-general, and another poundage of 5 per cent. on the expenditure of those monies, make it the interest of that officer, to fell the timber and to promote and enhance the expence of repairs and works in the forests. The whole of the actual business in the forests being transacted by deputies, and those deputies not acting upon oath ; the sales of the wood and timber, being wholly under their direction, without any adequate check or control ; and those deputies in many instances, (as appear by our former reports) the buyers of the wood and timber themselves ; the works and repairs, being either performed by them, or by workmen of their appointment, upon estimates of their own forming ; and neither those estimates made on oath, nor the works afterwards surveyed, or the accounts sworn to, by those who transact the business. Though the surveyor-general himself is accountable on oath, he must leave the whole entirely dependent on the personal integrity of an individual, who is neither from rank, situation, or the fair emoluments of office, placed above the temptation of ordinary corruption, and yet this officer is the only one who has any special charge of the growing timber in the forests."

The report goes on to state, that the stools or roots of the trees felled, which unquestionably belong to the Crown, are here taken by the keepers. Thus Mr. John Bull, who, it may reasonably be presumed, has some little interest in the concern, is compelled to pay foreign merchants for timber when he could partly grow it himself. And witness the devouring spoilation of the tenants of his forests by lords and lacqueys in office, who insultingly tell him, " he has nothing to do with the *laws* but to *obey them*."

The fox-hunting establishment of the Duke of Grafton is kept up with considerable spirit at Sholbrook, two miles from Wakefield-lodge, a delightful seat in the heart of the forest, the residence of General Fitzroy.

Sportsmen, who are partial to the chase, will find this one of the pleasantest and best adapted counties in England for hunting, being so little intersected with rivers, and for the most part an open country.

Three miles onward brought us to Stony Stratford, which (having noticed before) we passed through, and on the right, at a short distance, leave the village of Passenham, and the celebrated church of Calverton. The scenery now became very interesting, and we had a noble back-ground in the views of the three Brick-hills

on the opposite side of Fenny Stratford. The next spot
we passed through was Shenley, on either side of which,
and on elevations, are the churches of that parish and
Loughton, both very interesting objects. At six miles
from Stony we again pass through Fenny Stratford, but
in another direction to the former way we entered it,
crossing the navigation of the canal by the high road up
to Little Brick-hill, which is a pleasant and picturesque
village, situate on the top of one of the highest hills that
the Watling-street leads over, in our present route. Here,
taking the road to the right in an easterly direction,
for Great Brick-hill, where we entered upon a desart
of sand ; nothing short of the fine scenery, viewed from
its brow, would tempt us again to cross so disagreeable
a road. A horse, in dry weather, sinks half way to his
knees in sand at every step, and this continues all the
way to Leighton Beaudesert, a distance of five miles from
Little Brick-hill. Rounding the cap of Brick-hill Magna,
we come to the mansion of Mr. Duncombe. The views
from this hill and all the way to Leighton, present a noble
tract of fine and extensive scenery, and well repaid our
disagreeable road. We pass the village of Heath, and
from the termination of the hill look down on the town
we are about to enter. This eminence embraces an entire
view of the valley from Fenny Stratford to Leighton ;
an opening presents itself, at the entrance of the
opposite vale, and introduces an expanse of scenery all
the way to Ivingho and Marsworth, with the hills of
Ashridge and Penley in the extreme distance. A second
scene, on declining the hill towards Leighton, introduced
to our view a very sweet effect of the navigation, coursing
its way from the lower parts of the valley, and gradually
rising to our sight by the help of its locks; with charming
accompaniments on either bank, of woods and rich har-

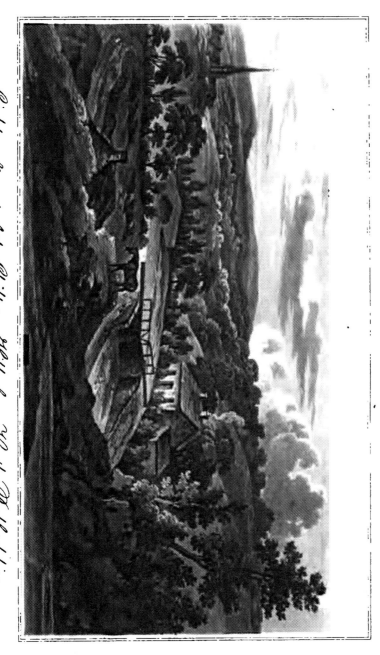

Leighton & part of the Chiltern Hills, from Heath, Bedfordshire.

Drawn by I. Hassell

London Pub.d 1 Augt 1819 by I. Hassell, 15 Richard .....

vest fields, the town is seen on a rising ground on one
side, and a moderate hill opposed to it on the other, while
the valley opening behind, terminates, as just before observed, by the distances of Ashridge and Penley.

We crossed the top of Leighton town, which we have
before-described, and descend its southern brow into the
common fields, and at two miles passed through the village
of Billington, from whence the road leads by Northall-
bridge, over the little river Lovat, where the counties
of Bedfordshire and Buckinghamshire divide. At this
spot we come to a distant view of Eddlesborough church,
situated very singularly upon the top of a small hill or
mound, rising immediately from the valley. It makes a
remarkable appearance, and has the effect of a large
tumuli. The church is rather spacious for so small
a village; it has a moderate sized tower at the west end,
with an elegant light spire on its top, and, like the body
of the church, has pointed Gothic windows; its situation
commands the Icening road, and part of the Chiltern
Hills, which passes at its back; and skirts the valley all
the way to Tring in a south-west direction, with the hills
of Mentmore and Layburn to the west; it also commands the celebrated Roman way from Gaddesdon to
Aylesbury, which, emerging from between these hills,
would make Eddlesborough, from its situation, appear as
a Roman guard way, or a second sort of look-out station,
in the chancel are some brasses of a large size, among which
is that of Sir John Swynshide, rector of Eddlesborough,
who died in 1390; in the north chancel, or Rufford aisle,
are some tombs of the family of Rufford.

The village of Eddlesborough is very pleasantly situated on the brow of the hill which the church stands upon.

The Earl of Bridgewater is patron of the vicarage
and impropriator of the great tithes, which belonged

formerly to the monks of the Charter-house. The parish church register records the burial of Michael Fenn, at the great age of 124, April 21, 1675. Northall and Dagnall are hamlets of this parish.

At some distance beyond Eddlesborough, we cross the Icening-way, and gradually rise into a very pleasant country until we reach Dagnall, another village; from whence we pass by a cross-road through the fields to Little Gaddesden. We had occasionally seen a deal of game in our route, but here the fields were literally covered with them; the evening had far advanced, and the pheasants were feeding before us, and crowing in woods on either side; hares were in every field, and on the brow of a hill the multitude of rabbits reminded us of a warren. A superabundance of game is the farmer's pest, and a country's worst friend; it is a temptation to the idle, and a sure invitation to the poacher. Our game laws are a disgrace to the country—the farmer that feeds the *fera natura*, formerly the property of the holder of the soil, is generally debarred from killing them, though they should ruin him; and he has also the superlative prospect of being shot at by a spring-gun, or caught in a steel-trap, if he should enter a copse of his own, contrary to the will of the lord of the manor. With a rising moon, we entered Little Gaddesdon, or Gadausdon Parva, a pleasant village, with a comfortable inn, the Bridgewater Arms, where we slept. On the following morning, before breakfast, we visited the church, which stands about half a mile eastward of our quarters. The view from the church-yard is extensive and diversified, overlooking the country we had passed the evening before. We could clearly discern the Icening-way, under the Chiltern Hills, and Eddlesborough rising in the vale beneath; the Horton Hills closed up the distance, the downs, nearer the sight,

rise in bold forms, with excellent pasturage and woods
on their sides, and some wood towards their summits.
The church is very antique, though small, and contains
several monuments.   Our principal object here was a
visit to Ashridge, the seat of the Earl of Bridgewater.

Ashridge-house is a short mile distant from the inn;
the entrance is through a swing-gate, from whence the
path leads by a steep ascent into one of the ash groves,
for which these grounds are so celebrated, and from the
immense number that grow here, the place originally
took its name.   Camden says, " it was formerly a royal
seat, and worthy to be so now for its beauty and com-
modiousness.   Here was anciently a religious house,
built by Edmund, Earl of Cornwall, for a new sort of
monks of the order of St. Austin, called Bon Hommes;
but since their suppression, it has become the seat of the
Egertons, Earl of Bridgewater.   It stands in the midst
of a park, five miles in compass, well wooded and stocked
with deer, with a fine *vista* across it.   The country round
it is extremely pleasant, and affords great conveniency
for sporting, which renders this seat a delightful retirement, from whence the prospect is of the vale of Aylesbury."   Camden continues his ecclesiastical account by
observing, "the Bon Hommes were a reformed sort of
Benedictines, founded by Edmund, the son of Richard,
Earl of Cornwall, and King of the Romans, 5 Edward I.
There was but one house more of this order in England,
and that was at Edington, in Wiltshire.   They were to
consist of one rector and twenty brethren, of which
thirteen at least were to be priests.   It was erected in
honour of the precious blood of Jesus Christ, of which a
small parcel (as the monks pretended) was kept here.
He gave to it his manor of Asheridge, or Ashereig, with
divers other lands, possessions, liberties, and privileges,

as to be free from all toll and scutage, and that neither
he nor his heirs should interpose in the business of the
house, but at the death of the rector, they should have
the custody of it, and have liberty to chuse another, without presenting him to the patron. It was valued, at the
Suppression, at £416 6s. 4d. per annum, by Dugdale;
and £447 18s. 2d. by Speed. A parliament was held at
Ashridge, in the reign of Edward I. In 1554, Elizabeth,
becoming the avowed object of Queen Mary's hatred,
and being openly treated with disrespect and insult,
thought it most prudent to leave the court, and retire to
her house at Ashridge; during which time she was accompanied by Sir Thomas Pope and others, more as
spies than attendants. It was from this place she was
dragged out of a sick bed, and carried on a litter to London by command of Mary, who ordered Sir Edward
Hastings, Sir Thomas Cornwall, and Sir Edward South-
well, by a peremptory commission, to bring her to court,
where she was closely confined by Mary. After her re-
lease she changed her country abode from this place to
Hatfield."

The present building of Ashridge-house was begun
by the late Duke of Bridgewater, from plans and
drawings by the late celebrated Mr. Wyatt. It is a cas-
tellated building, with corner towers, and a projecting
central front, with a tower rising from the centre of the
building. The north-west front, which presents itself
on entering the park in this direction, is certainly very
imposing, and strikes the beholder with admiration;
but on a closer advance there is something little. By
introducing a range of contemptible apartments between
the ground floor and the upper rooms, the pigmy
windows, attached to them, ruin the effect, and destroy
the grandeur that would otherwise be predominant.

For what purpose Mr. Wyatt destroyed this noble design, is beyond our conjecture ; it is so, and stands a record of littleness in the centre of grandeur. The chapel, at the farthest extremity, is an elegant and light building, with a handsome tower, surmounted with an octagon spire. The design, which is partly Gothic, is a perfect model of taste and workmanship. The main body of the building is connected with its projecting wings by a suite of apartments on each side, diversified in appearance. Here, indeed, some apology can be offered for the small windows surmounting the large ones, as the top of the building comes to a termination, beside which, it is only a dependent part—not so with the grand front. The beauty of the face of Ashridge-house is cut up, in effect, by the middle suit of apartments.

Our annexed drawing was taken from the high ash grove, on the left. As we advanced towards the house, and just as we had finished our sketch—" Anon, a careless herd, full of the pasture, jumps along," followed by three fat bucks, marked to die, and pursued by two park-keepers on horseback, with their rifle guns. Having seen this operation so often, and not much inclined to risk an accident, we withdrew, and returned to our quarters.

In Little Gaddesdon rises the river Gade, at first simply a brook ; from whence it gradually assumes some import, and becomes a treasure to the millers and paper-makers on its stream. The road continues by the side of the park for some distance ; after which we pass Nettleton, a village pleasantly situate between hills. Soon we came in view of Gaddesden-place, the seat of Mrs. Halsey, the widow of the late member for St. Alban's. The house is pleasantly seated on the highest part of the park, and commands very extensive prospects. It is built much

in the style of the villas after Palladio's designs, with a
portico in front, supported by Corinthian columns. The
grounds are laid out with taste, and there is an abundance of wood and plantations in the park. The Gade
river now courses by the side of the road, and becomes
a broad sheet of water. A continuance of rural scenery
accompanies us until we pass the seat of Astley Cooper,
esq. a delightful spot, on the summit of a hill on our
right, just before we entered Hamel Hampsted.

Hamel Hampsted is a town celebrated in the time of
the Saxons, who called it Henamstead, or Hean Hampsted, signifying High Hampsted. After the Conquest, it
obtained the name of Hamelamstcole, and is since altered
to its present name. Henry VIII. granted it a charter of
incorporation, vesting the government in the hands of a
bailiff, &c. empowering the corporation to use a common
seal, and hold a pie-powder court, during its markets
and fair. The wheat market here is reckoned the first in
the county. Much advantage has accrued to this town
from its contiguity to the Grand Junction navigation.
Hamel Hempsted stands an incontrovertible fact of the
great benefits resulting from inland navigation—its trade
having increased in three-fold ratio within the last thirty
years. At the bottom of the town is Bury-house, a remarkable pleasant mansion, and where the owner of the
manor, John Waterhouse, esq. in the reign of Hen. VIII.
entertained that monarch. This estate, though only consisting of twenty-four acres and a half, includes the entire town of Hemel Hempsted, which is situate on the
brow of a hill inclining downwards to the river Gade;
it consists of one principal street, with some of minor
consideration, branching from it. The corporation have
erected a new market-house, which is built from a
respectable design, and is partly brick, with the central

Batchworth Mills.— Herts.

Drawn by J. Hassell

projection of a stone facing. The church is a very picturesque object; rising immediately from behind the market-house, with a lofty spire, it gives a pleasant finish to
the town, breaking the line of buildings, and is an object
of importance between the two hills that shelter the houses
on either side. As we leave this town, and on the right
at the bridge, which the road leads over towards Berk-
hampstead, there is a choice piece of scenery, looking
down the navigation that traverses Box Moor, towards
Bourn-end and Broad-way. Returning from Two
Waters by the road on the left of the canal, we have
a varied ride, through the scenery we have described
before in our route downwards, from Hunton bridge,
by King's Langley, to Box Moor. With a smart pace
we reached Watford in an hour. We have so thoroughly detailed all that belongs to this town, that we
had only to pass on to the course of the Grand Junction,
in our way to the capital. At the southern extremity of
Cashiobury-park, the seat of the Earl of Essex, we
again fall in with that stream. In ascending the brow
of the next hill, we perceive the junction of the river
Colne with the Gade, and the opposite side of the valley
presents us with a view of the celebrated silk mills; they
are conducted on a very superior principal, and have recently been extended and repaired. From thence the
river Colne and the Junction streams are seen winding
through the vale of Watford to the Moor waters, passing
Messrs. Smith and Son's paper mills, and then gliding
under Moor Park woods; to Batchworth mills. Towards
evening this is a very imposing and grand scene.*

* For a particular account of Moor Park, &c. see the author's work, entitled Picturesque Rides and Walks Thirty Miles round London.

L

There is a little inn at Batchworth, kept by a butcher as well as vintner, and where twice in my life I have dined off the best mutton chops I ever tasted, and the good landlady adds civility to the qualities of an excellent cook, who can dress a chop equal to the first tavern in London, carefully attending to give them to us hot from the fire.

Turning round by the Bear inn, we take the road to Harefield, and at the summit of the hill have a delightful view into the valley with the town of Rickmansworth in its farthest recess. About a mile to the right and descending to the Colne stream, are some celebrated copper mills; and at the extremity of the village, we come in view of a charming expanse of scenery, the Colne and the navigation passing up the vale beneath us, the river meandering in a variety of curves, wanders under the opposite brows, which are bounded by some noble woods in the distance; beyond this the hills rise in bold forms, delineating a very sweet picture.

As we decline the hill, the church, a rural object, stands a short distance on the left. From this place the road passes between hedge-rows, and we have only occasional peeps into the valley; at four miles and a half from Harefield, we enter

Uxbridge—From this town we took our departure for Cowley, to view the gauge-locks which correspond with those of the same description at the Cow-roast. The country here becomes open and pleasant, we now continued on the tow-path of the canal to Philpot-bridge, and then by Pickwell to Bullbridge, where the Paddington canal unites with the Grand Junction. The next place we pass is Bluebridge, and then to Norwood; here the scenery begins to resume its former interest, the canal passes onwards by Osterly Park,* from whence it glides by Sion-Hill Park and enters the river Thames at Old Brentford.

* For an account of Osterly House, &c. see the author's work of Pictu-resque Rides and Walks Thirty Miles round London.

INDEX.

INDEX.

INDEX.

DIRECTIONS

FOR

PLACING THE CUTS.